Contents

W9-APH-017

1 Introduction

Mac computers are renowned for their ease-of-use, stability and security, with good reason. They are an excellent option for anyone, particularly senior users, since they usually do exactly what is required of them, in a fun, effective way too.

Life and Times of Apple

Apple, the makers of Mac computers, was founded in California in 1976 by Steve Jobs, Steve Wozniak and Ronald Wayne. Originally called Apple Computer the initial emphasis of the company was very much on personal computers. After some innovative early machines, Steve Jobs decided that the next Apple computer had to have a Graphical User Interface (GUI). This is a computer that can be controlled by the user with a device such as a mouse or a joystick. In many ways this was the breakthrough that has shaped the modern face of personal computing.

The first Macintosh computer, using a GUI, was released in 1984. The sales of the first Mac were good, particularly because of its strength using graphics and for desktop publishing. However, shortly afterwards Steve Jobs left Apple which was the beginning of a downturn for the company. Although the introduction of the first PowerBook was a success, the increasing development of Microsoft Windows and IBM-compatible PCs became a real threat to the existence of Apple.

The rise of the iMac

During the 1990s, Apple experienced several commercial setbacks and the company was in trouble. However, shortly afterwards Steve Jobs returned to Apple and in 1998, the iMac was launched. Apple had always been known for its stylish design but the iMac took this to a new level. With its all-in-one design and bright, translucent colors it transformed people's attitudes towards personal computers.

The iMac got Apple back on its commercial feet and this was followed in 2001 by the iPod, a portable digital music player. Like the iMac this caught the public's imagination and Apple has exploited this with dramatic effect with the addition of products such as iTunes, iPhone, iPad and its OS X operating system. The death of Steve Jobs in October 2011 created a potential challenge for Apple but his legacy, in terms of the range of innovative products that he introduced, has left it strongly positioned in the market.

Don't forget

Mac users are usually very devoted to the Apple brand and support it with very enthusiastic fervor.

Choosing a Mac

As with most things in the world of technology there is a wide range of choice when it comes to buying a Mac computer. This includes the top-of-the-range Mac Pro, which is a very powerful desktop computer, to the MacBook Air, which is a laptop that is thin enough to fit into an envelope – if required! In between these two extremes is a variety of desktops and laptops that can match most people's computing needs. For the senior user some of the best options are:

Desktop
As a good, all-purpose, desktop computer the iMac is hard to beat. This is the machine that helped to turn around Apple's fortunes in the 1990s and it remains one of its most popular computers.

The iMac is a self-contained computer which means the hard drive and the monitor are housed together as a single unit. There is a variety of models that offer different levels of computing power and different monitor sizes. At the time of writing, all models have a DVD writer and come with wireless connectivity for connection to the Internet.

Another desktop option is the Mac Mini, which is a smaller, cheaper, computer that consists of just the hard drive. This means that you have to buy the mouse, keyboard and monitor separately. This is a reasonable option if your computing needs are mainly email, the Internet and word processing. For anything more, the iMac is a better option.

Laptop
More and more people are using laptops these days, as mobile computing takes over from static desktops. In the Mac range, the MacBook is probably the best all-round option. Although not as powerful as the iMac, it has enough computing power for most people's needs. The MacBook Pro comes in a standard model and also a Retina Display screen version with a higher resolution screen. The MacBook Air is ultra-thin and a great option for when traveling.

The Mac Operating System

The Mac operating system (the software that is the foundation of how the computer works) is known as OS X (pronounced "ten"). This is now on version 10.8, which is more commonly known as Mountain Lion.

Apple is renowned for designing operating systems that are easy to use, robust and more secure than their Windows-based PC counterparts. The OS X operating system is based on UNIX, a system that is both secure and has stood the test of time.

OS X is not only easy to use it also has a very attractive graphical interface. This is created by a technology known as Quartz and the interface itself is known as Aqua, which is a set of graphics based on the theme of water.

The OS X Mountain Lion interface is immediately eye-catching as soon as any Mac is turned on:

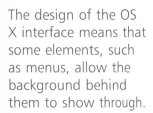

Ports and Slots Explained

Every Mac computer has a number of ports and slots for different functions to be performed or additional devices to be attached.

DVD/CD slot

This is the slot into which DVDs or CDs can be inserted to play their content. It can also be used to burn content onto blank DVDs or CDs. This slot is at the side or front of the computer, depending on the type and model of the Mac.

USB ports

These are the ports that are used to connect a variety of external devices such as digital cameras, memory card readers, pen drives or external hard drives. On most Macs there is a minimum of two USB ports.

Firewire ports

These are similar to USB ports but they are generally used for devices that are required to transfer larger amounts of data. One of the most common uses for Firewire is the transfer of digital video. Firewire ports look similar to USB ports except they are slightly chunkier.

Thunderbolt

This is a port for transferring data at high speeds, up to 12 times faster than Firewire. It can also be used to connect a Thunderbolt screen to a MacBook.

Ethernet

This is for the connection of an Ethernet cable, for a cable or broadband Internet connection.

The Mac Desktop

The first thing to do with your new Mac is to turn it on. This is done by pressing this button once (this is for a standard MacBook).

Don't forget

The On button for the MacBook Air and MacBook Retina Display is located on the keyboard itself, rather than in the top-right corner. On an iMac the On button is at the back of the display.

The first thing you will see is the Mac desktop. This is the default layout and, as we will see in the next few pages, this can be customized to your own preferences.

Some of the specific elements of the desktop are:

Don't forget

If the Finder is not showing, click on this icon on the Dock. The Dock is the collection of icons at the bottom of the screen.

Apple Menu   Finder Menu bars

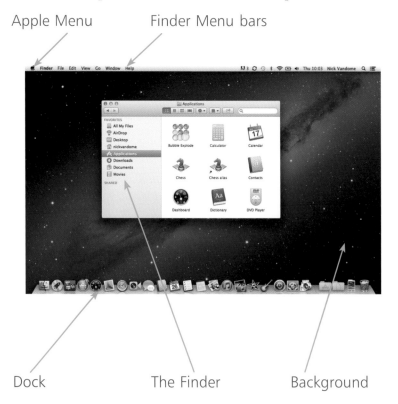

Dock   The Finder   Background

Customizing Your Mac

All of us have different ideas about the way we want our computers set up, in terms of layout, colors, size and graphics. Macs allow a great deal of customization so that you can personalize yours to genuinely make it feel like your own computer.

The customization features are contained within the System Preferences. To access these:

1 Click here on the Dock (the full workings of the Dock will be covered in detail in Chapter Two)

2 The System Preferences folder contains a variety of functions that can be used to customize your Mac (see following pages for details)

Hot tip

Click on the Show All button at the top of the System Preferences folder to show all of the items in the folder, regardless of which element you are currently using.

Changing the Background

Background imagery is an important way to add your own personal touch to your Mac. (This is the graphical element upon which all other items on your computer sit.) There are a range of background options that can be used. To select your own background:

1 Click on this icon in the System Preferences folder

Desktop & Screen Saver

2 Click on the Desktop tab

Desktop

3 Select a location from where you want to select a background

▼Apple
📁 Desktop Pictures
📁 Nature
📁 Plants
📁 Art
📁 Black & White
📁 Abstract
📁 Patterns
⚪ Solid Colors

4 Click on one of the available backgrounds

5 The background is applied as the desktop background imagery

14

Changing the Screen Saver

A screen saver is the element that appears when the Mac has not been used for a specified period of time. Originally this was designed to avoid screen burn (caused by items being at the same position on the screen for an extended period of time) but now they largely consist of a graphical element. To select your own screen saver:

1 Click on this button in the System Preferences folder

2 Click on the Screen Saver tab

3 Select an option here for a slideshow screen saver, or

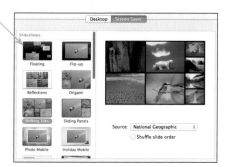

Don't forget

The slideshow screen saver consists of different images that appear as tiles on the screen.

4 Scroll down to access other Screen Saver Options

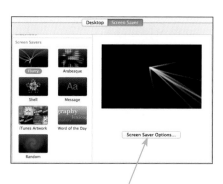

5 Click the Screen Saver Options… button to select options for the way the screen saver operates

Changing the Screen Size

For most computer users the size at which items are displayed on the screen is a crucial issue: if items are too small this can make them hard to read and lead to eye strain; too large and you have to spend a lot of time scrolling around to see everything.

The size of items on the screen is controlled by the screen's resolution, i.e. the number of colored dots displayed in an area of the screen. The higher the resolution the smaller the items on the screen, the lower the resolution the larger the items. To change the screen resolution:

Don't forget

A higher resolution makes items appear sharper on the screen, even though they appear physically smaller.

16

1 Click on this button in the System Preferences folder

Displays

2 Click on the Display tab **Display**

3 Click on the Best for built-in display button to let your Mac select the most appropriate resolution

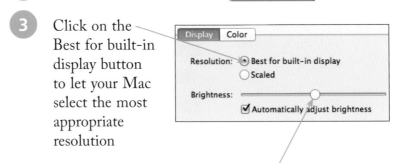

4 Drag this slider to change the screen brightness. Check on the box to have this done automatically

5 Click on the Scaled button and select a resolution setting to change the overall screen resolution

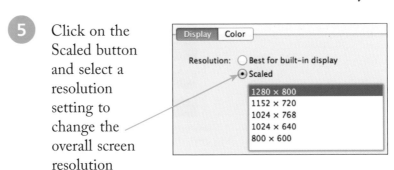

Making Things Accessible

In all areas of computing it is important to give as many people access to the system as possible. This includes users with visual impairments and also people who have problems using the mouse and keyboard. In OS X this is achieved through the functions of the Accessibility System Preferences. To use these:

1 Click on this button in the System Preferences folder

2 Click on the Display button for options for changing the display colors, contrast and increasing the cursor size

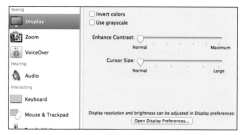

3 Click on the Zoom button for options to zoom in on the screen

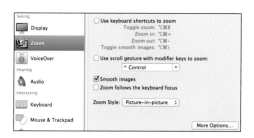

4 Click on the VoiceOver button to enable VoiceOver, which provides a spoken description of what is on the screen

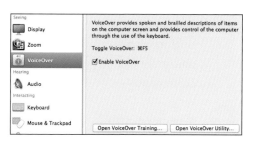

Don't forget

Experiment with the VoiceOver function if only to see how it operates. This will give you a better idea of how visually-impaired users access information on a computer.

...cont'd

5 Click on the Audio button to select an on-screen flash for alerts and how sound is played

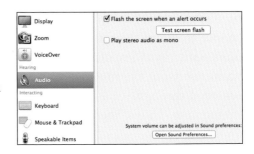

6 Click on the Keyboard button to access options for customizing the keyboard

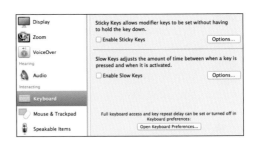

Don't forget

The Audio, Keyboard, and Mouse & Trackpad accessibility options have links to additional options within their own System Preferences.

7 Click on the Mouse & Trackpad button to access options for customizing these devices

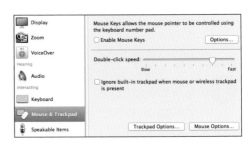

8 Click on the Speakable Items button to select options for using spoken commands

9 Check on this button to enable assistive technology such as screen readers

The Spoken Word

Mountain Lion not only has numerous options for adding text to documents, emails and messages; it also has a dictation function so that you can speak what you want to appear on screen. To set up and use the dictation feature:

1 Click on this button in the System Preferences folder

2 By default, Dictation is Off

3 Check on the On button to enable dictation

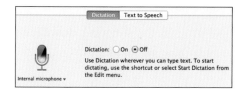

Hot tip

Punctuation can be added with the dictation function, by speaking commands such as 'comma' or 'question mark'. These will then be converted into the appropriate symbols.

4 Click on the Enable Dictation button

5 Once Dictation has been turned On, it can be accessed in relevant apps by selecting Edit>Start Dictation from the menu bar

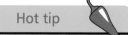

6 Start talking when the microphone icon appears. Click Done when you have finished recording your text

7 Click on the Text to Speech tab to make selections for dictation

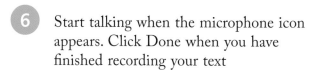

Shutting Down and Sleeping

When you are not using your Mac you will want to either shut it down or put it to sleep. If you shut it down this may close all of your applications and open files. This is the best option if you are not going to be returning to your Mac for a reasonable length of time (say, more than one day).

If you put the Mac to sleep, it will retain your current work session so that you can continue when you wake up the Mac. This option is useful if you know you will be returning to your Mac within a few hours.

The process for shutting down or putting a Mac to sleep is very similar in both cases:

1 Click on this icon on the main Menu bar

2 Click on either Sleep or Shut Down...

Hot tip

Check on the 'Reopen windows when logging back in' box when you shut down. This ensures that the next time you turn on your Mac, it will resume at the place where you closed it, i.e. all open apps and files will appear in their previous state.

20

3 If you are shutting down, a window appears asking you to confirm your request

Are you sure you want to shut down your computer now?

If you do nothing, the computer will shut down automatically in 36 seconds.

☑ Reopen windows when logging back in

Cancel   Shut Down

4 Click on the Shut Down button

2 Finding Your Way Around

This chapter looks at two of the vital elements on the Mac, the Finder and the Dock. It shows how to use these to access and view items. It also shows how to work with different windows and organize your desktop. It also covers some new ways to navigate with your computer and introduces the Mac App Store.

Finder: the Core of Your Mac

One of the most basic requirements of any computer is that you can easily and quickly find the applications and documents which you want to use. On Macs, a lot of this work is done through the aptly-named Finder. This is the area on your Mac which you can use to store, organize and display files, folders and applications. It is an area that you will return to frequently whenever you are using your Mac. To access the Finder:

Don't forget

By default a home folder is created in the Finder when you first set up your Mac. This will contain all of your own folders and files. Some of these folders will also be in the Finder Sidebar. These are just shortcuts to these items.

1 Click on this icon on the Dock (this is one element of the Dock that cannot be removed)

2 The Finder window has a Sidebar and a main window area

3 The Sidebar can be used to create folders and categories for a variety of items

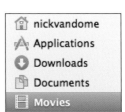

Hot tip

The first link on the Finder Sidebar is All My Files. This lists all of the latest files that have been created or saved to your Mac. This is an excellent way to view your most recent files.

4 The main window displays items within the selected location

Using the Sidebar

The Sidebar is the left-hand panel of the Finder which can be used to access items on your Mac:

1 Click on a button on the Sidebar

2 Its contents are displayed in the main Finder window

23

Adding to the Sidebar

Items that you access most frequently can be added to the Sidebar. To do this:

1 Drag an item from the main Finder window onto the Sidebar

2 The item is added to the Sidebar. You can do this with apps, folders and files

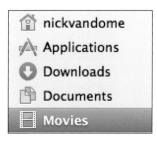

...cont'd

Viewing items in the Finder

Items within the Finder can be viewed in a number of different ways:

Hot tip

In Icons view it is possible to view the icons at different sizes. To do this, click on the wheel icon next to the view icon and select Show View Options. Then drag the Icon size slider for the appropriate size.

1   Click on this button to view items as icons

2   Click on this button to view items as a list

3   Click on this button to view items in columns

Quick Look

Through a Finder option called Quick Look, it is possible to view the content of a file without having to first open it.
To do this:

1 Select a file within the Finder

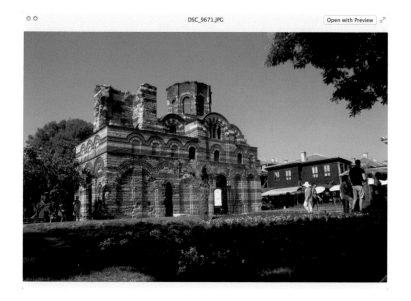

DSC_9669.JPG
DSC_9670.JPG
DSC_9671.JPG
DSC_9672.JPG
DSC_9673.JPG

2 Press the space bar

3 The contents of the file are displayed without it opening in its default app

4 Click on the cross to close Quick Look

0 1021 0281407 0

Covers

Covers is an innovative feature on the Mac that enables you to view the contents of a folder without having to open the folder. Additionally, each item is displayed as a large icon that enables you to see what a particular item contains, such as images. To use Covers:

1 Select a folder and at the top of the Finder window click on this button

2 The items within the folder are displayed in their cover state

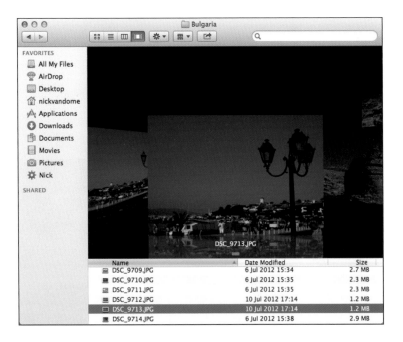

3 Drag with the mouse on each item to view the next one, or click on the slider at the bottom of the window

Using the Dock

The Dock is the collection of icons that, by default, appears along the bottom of the desktop. If you choose, this can stay visible permanently. The Dock is a way to quickly access the apps and folders that you use most frequently. The two main things to remember about the Dock are:

- It is divided into two: apps go on the left of the dividing line; all other items go on the right

- It can be edited in just about any way you choose

Hot tip

Items on the Dock can be activated by clicking on them once, rather than double-clicking.

By default, the Dock appears at the bottom of the screen, but it can also be positioned at the left- or right-hand side of the screen (see page 28)

...cont'd

Customizing the Dock

The Dock can be modified in numerous ways. This can affect both the appearance of the Dock and the way it operates. To set Dock preferences:

Don't forget

The Apple Menu is accessed from the Apple icon that is always visible at the top left of the screen.

Beware

If you select the Turn Hiding On option for the Dock then it is hidden unless you pass the cursor over the bottom of the screen (or wherever it is hidden). However, this can become annoying as the Dock then appears and disappears at times you do not want it to.

1 Select Apple Menu>Dock from the Menu bar

2 Select one of the options for how the Dock is displayed on the screen

Turn Hiding On	⌥⌘D
Turn Magnification On	
Position on Left	
✓ Position on Bottom	
Position on Right	
Dock Preferences...	

3 Click on Dock Preferences... to access more options for customizing the Dock

Dock Preferences...

4 Check on the Magnification box and drag this slider to specify how much larger an icon becomes when the cursor is passed over it

Adding and removing items

To add items to the Dock:

1 For apps, drag their icon onto the Dock, to the left of the dividing line

Don't forget

Removing items from the Dock does not remove them from your Mac. The items on the Dock are only a reference to the actual locations of the items.

2 For folders or files, drag their icon onto the Dock, to the right of the dividing line

3 To remove items from the Dock, drag them off the Dock and they will disappear in a satisfying puff of smoke

Dock menus

Each Dock item has its own contextual menu that has commands relevant to that item. To access these:

Don't forget

If an app window is closed, the app remains open and the window is placed within the app icon on the Dock. If an item is minimized it goes on the right of the Dock dividing line.

1 Click and hold beneath a Dock item

2 The contextual menu is displayed next to the Dock item. Click on a command as required

...cont'd

Stacking items

To save space on the Dock it is possible to add folders to the Dock, from where their contents can be accessed. This is known as Stacks. By default, Stacks for documents and downloaded files are created on the Dock. To use Stacks:

1 Stacked items are placed at the right-hand side of the Dock

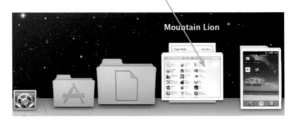

2 Click on a Stack to view its contents

3 Stacks can be viewed as a grid, or

4 As a fan, depending on the number of items it contains, or

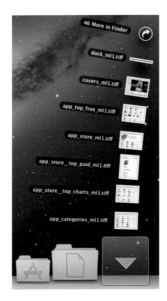

Hot tip

Move the cursor over a Stack and press Ctrl+click to access options for how that Stack is displayed.

5 As a list. Click on a folder to view its contents within a Stack. Click on files to open them in their relevant app

6 To create a new Stack, drag a folder onto the Dock. Any new items that are added to the folder will also be visible through the Stack

Mission Control

Mission Control is a function in OS X Mountain Lion that helps you organize all of your open apps, full-screen apps and documents. It also enables you to quickly view the Dashboard and Desktop. Within Mission Control there are also Spaces, where you can group together similar types of documents. To use Mission Control:

1 Click on this button on the Dock

2 All open files and apps are visible via Mission Control

3 Desktop items are grouped together on the top row within Mission Control within an area called a Space. Position the cursor over the right-hand corner and click on the plus sign to add a new Space. Drag items from the desktop onto the new Space

32

4 If there is more than one window open for an app they will be grouped together by Mission Control

Safari

5 If an app is made full-screen (see pages 40–41) it automatically appears along the top row

Safari   Calendar

Beware

Any apps or files that have been minimized or closed do not appear within the main Mission Control window. Instead they are located to the right of the dividing line on the Dock.

Working with Mac Windows

When you are working with a lot of open windows it can sometimes be confusing about which is the active window and how you can then quickly switch to other windows.

1 The active window always sits on the top of any other open windows. There can only be one active window at any one time

2 Click on any window behind the currently active one, to bring it to the front and make it active

3 At the top left of any active window, click on the red button to close it, the amber button to minimize it and the green button to enlarge it

Launchpad

Even though the Dock can be used to store shortcuts to your applications, it is limited in terms of space. The full set of applications on your Mac can be found in the Finder but OS X Mountain Lion has a feature that allows you to quickly access and manage all of your applications. These include the ones that are pre-installed on your Mac and also any that you install yourself or download from the Apple App Store. This feature is called Launchpad. To use it:

1. Click once on this button on the Dock

Don't forget

To launch an app from within Launchpad, click on it once.

2. All of the apps are displayed

3. Similar types of apps can be grouped together in individual folders. By default, the Utilities are grouped in this way

Utilities

Mac Apps

In addition to the Launchpad, Mac programs (apps) are located in the Applications folder. This is located within the Finder. To view and access the available apps:

1 Click on the Applications button in the Finder

Hot tip

Apps can be added to the Dock by dragging their icons there from the Applications folder.

2 The currently-installed apps are displayed

3 To open an app, double-click on its icon

The App Store

The App Store is another OS X app. This is an online facility where you can download and buy new apps. These cover a range of categories such as productivity, business and entertainment. When you select or buy an app from the App Store, it is downloaded automatically by Launchpad and appears here next to the rest of the apps.

To buy apps from the App Store you need to have an Apple ID and account. If you have not already set this up, it can be done when you first access the App Store. To use the App Store:

1 Click on this icon on the Dock or within the Launchpad

2 The homepage of the App Store contains the current top-featured apps

3 Your account information and Quick Link categories are listed at the right-hand side of the page

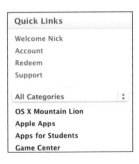

Downloading Apps

The App Store contains a wide range of apps: from small, fun apps, to powerful productivity ones. However, downloading them from the App Store is the same regardless of the type of app. The only differences are whether they require payment or not and the length of time they take to download. To download an app from the App Store:

1 Browse through the App Store until you find the required app

38

2 Click on the app to view a detailed description about it

3 Click on the button underneath the app icon to download it. If there is no charge for the app the button will say "Free"

4 If there is a charge for the app, the button will say "Buy App"

5 Click on the Install App button

6 Enter your Apple ID account details to continue downloading the app

7 The progress of the download is displayed in a progress bar underneath the Launchpad icon on the Dock

8 Once it has been downloaded, the app is available within Launchpad

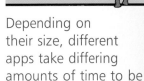

Don't forget

Depending on their size, different apps take differing amounts of time to be downloaded.

Don't forget

As you download more apps, additional pages will be created within the Launchpad to accommodate them.

Full-Screen Apps

When working with apps we all like to be able to see as much of a window as possible. With OS X Mountain Lion this is possible with the full-screen app functionality. This allows you to expand an app with this feature so that it takes up the whole of your monitor or screen with a minimum of toolbars visible. Some apps have this functionality but some do not. To use full-screen apps:

 By default an app appears on the desktop with other windows behind it

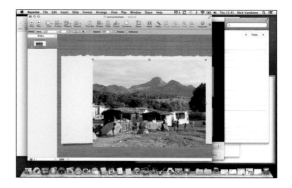

 Don't forget

If the button in Step 2 is not visible then the app does not have the full-screen functionality.

 Click on this button at the top right-hand corner of the app's window

 The app is expanded to take up the whole window. The main Apple Menu bar and the Dock are hidden

4 To view the
main Menu
bar, move the
cursor over the
top of the screen

5 You can move between all full-screen apps by
swiping with three fingers left or right on a trackpad
or Magic Mouse (see page 42)

6 Move the cursor over the top right-hand
corner of the screen and click on this button
to close the full-screen functionality

7 In Mission Control all of the open full-screen apps
are shown in the top row

A New Way of Navigating

One of the most revolutionary features of OS X Mountain Lion is the way in which you can navigate around your applications, web pages and documents. This involves a much greater reliance on swiping on a trackpad or adapted mouse; techniques that have been imported from the iPhone and the iPad. These are known as multi-touch gestures and to take full advantage of these you will need to have one of the following devices:

- A trackpad. This will be found on MacBooks

- A Magic Trackpad. This can be used with an iMac, a Mac Mini or a Mac Pro. It works wirelessly via Bluetooth

- A Magic Mouse. This can be used with an iMac, a Mac Mini or a Mac Pro. It can also be used with a MacBook if desired. It works wirelessly via Bluetooth

All of these devices work using a swiping technique with fingers moving over their surface. This should be done with a light touch; it is a gentle swipe, and no pressure is applied to the device.

The trackpads and Magic Mouse do not have any buttons in the same way as traditional devices. Instead specific areas are clickable so that you can still perform left- and right-click operations.

No more scroll bars

Another feature in OS X Mountain Lion is the removal of scroll bars that are constantly visible on a web page or document. Instead, there are scroll bars that only appear when you are moving around a page or document. When you stop, the scroll bars melt way. Scrolling is done by multi-touch gestures on a trackpad or Magic Mouse.

By default, you can scroll through web pages or documents by swiping up or down with two fingers on a trackpad, Magic Trackpad or Magic Mouse. The full list of these multi-touch gestures is shown on page 45.

Don't forget

If you do not have a trackpad, a Magic Trackpad or a Magic Mouse you can still navigate within OS X Mountain Lion with a traditional mouse and scroll bars in windows.

Multi-Touch Preferences

Some multi-touch gestures only have a single action, which cannot be changed. However, others have options for changing the action for a specific gesture. This is done within the Trackpad preferences, where a full list of multi-touch gestures is shown:

Point & Click Preferences

1 Access the System Preferences and click on the Trackpad button

2 Click on the Point & Click tab

3 The actions are described on the left, with a graphic explanation on the right

Hot tip

When setting multi-touch preferences try to avoid having too many gestures using the same number of fingers, in case some of them override the others.

43

4 If there is a down arrow next to an option, click on it to change the way an action is activated

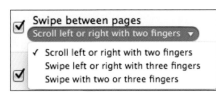

...cont'd

Scroll & Zoom Preferences

1 Click on the Scroll & Zoom tab **Scroll & Zoom**

2 The actions are described on the left, with a graphic explanation on the right

More Gestures Preferences

1 Click on the More Gestures tab **More Gestures**

2 The actions are described on the left, with a graphic explanation on the right

Multi-Touch Gestures

The list of trackpad multi-touch gestures are: (relevant ones for a Magic Mouse are in brackets)

Point & Click

- Tap to click – tap once with one finger (same for the Magic Mouse)

- Secondary click – click or tap with two fingers (single-click on the right of the Magic Mouse)

- Look up – double-tap with three fingers

- Three finger drag – move with three fingers

Scroll & Zoom

- Scroll direction – content tracks finger movement, with two fingers (one finger with the Magic Mouse)

- Zoom in or out – pinch or spread with two fingers

- Smart zoom – double-tap with two fingers (double-tap with one finger with the Magic Mouse)

- Rotate – rotate with two fingers

More Gestures

- Swipe between pages – scroll left or right with two fingers (scroll left or right with one finger with the Magic Mouse)

- Swipe between full-screen apps – swipe left or right with three fingers (swipe left or right with two fingers with the Magic Mouse)

- Access Mission Control – swipe up with three fingers (double-tap with two fingers with the Magic Mouse)

- Access Launchpad – pinch with thumb and three fingers

- Show Desktop – spread with thumb and three fingers

Removing Items

As you work on your Mac you will have some files, folders and apps that you definitely want to keep and others that you would like to remove. To do this:

1 In the Finder, click on the item you want to remove

malawi7.JPG

2 Drag it onto the Trash icon on the Dock

3 To empty all of the items from the Trash, select Finder>Empty Trash... from the Finder Menu bar

3 Organizing Your Mac

Keeping everything organized on a computer can sometimes be a bit of a headache. This chapter shows you how to work confidently with files and folders on your Mac and introduces some useful apps, such as those for creating an address book, making notes and setting reminders.

Creating Files

There are generally two ways for creating files on a Mac. One is to generate a new file within the app you are using and then save this into a folder. The other is to import files that have already been created, such as digital photographs.

Creating new files

The process for creating new files is essentially the same for all apps:

Don't forget

See Chapter Four for more information on working with digital photographs.

1 Open the app you want to use

2 Select File>New from the app's Menu bar

3 Depending on the app, there may be a properties window that can be used to define various elements of the file being created. Some apps also have templates that can be used as the basis of the document you want to create

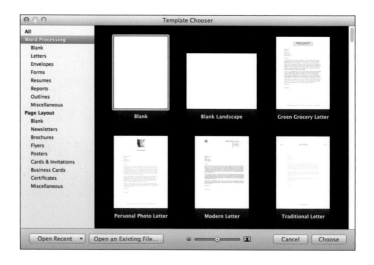

4 Add the required content to the file

Sharing Files

Next but one to the Actions button on the Finder is the Share button. This can be used to share a selected item, or items, in a variety of ways appropriate to the type of file that has been selected. For instance, a photo will have options including the photo-sharing site Flickr while a text document will have fewer options. To share items directly from the Finder:

2 Click on the Share button on the Finder toolbar and select one of the options

3 For some of the options, such as Twitter, Facebook and Flickr, you will be asked to add an account. If you already have an account you can enter the details or, if not, you can create a new account

Auto Save and Versions

One of the biggest causes of frustration when working with computers is if they crash and all of your unsaved work is lost. Luckily, with OS X Mountain Lion, losing unsaved material is now a thing of the past as it includes an Auto Save function that saves work in the background as you go along. This means that you do not have to worry about having unsaved documents.

Another function within Auto Save is Versions, which enables you to revert back to previous versions of a document. To do this:

1 Create a document with content

2 Select File>Save from the Menu bar

3 Edit the file

4 Click on the file name and select Browse All Versions...

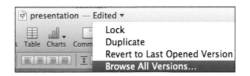

5 The current version is shown on the left-hand side and the previous versions on the right

Hot tip

To prevent any more changes being made to a document, click on the file name and click on Lock. To keep the current version and use another for editing, click on the Duplicate link.

6 Click on a previous version

51

7 Click on the Restore button

8 The previous version is restored as the current document

Opening Items

It is possible to open items on your Mac from the Dock or in the Finder.

From the Dock

1 Click on an item once to open it (app) or make it active (file)

In the Finder

1 Browse to the item you want to open

2 Double-click on the required item to open it

Creating a Folder Structure

As you create more and more files on your Mac it can become harder to find what you are looking for. To try and simplify this, it is a good idea to have a robust folder structure. This gives you a logical path to follow when you are looking for items. To create a folder structure:

① In the Finder, click on the Documents button

② In the main Finder window Ctrl+click and select New Folder

③ Enter a name for the new folder

OS X Mountain Lion

④ Double-click on the new folder to open it

⑤ Repeat Steps 2, 3 and 4 to create as much of a folder structure as required

Don't forget

Macs use spring-loaded folders. This means that if you drag a file over a folder and hold it there, the folder will automatically open. As long as you keep the mouse button held down, you can do this through as many layers as there are in a folder structure.

53

Compiling an Address Book

Having an address book on your Mac is an excellent way to keep track of your family and friends and it can also be used within other apps, such as the Mail app for email. To create an address book:

Don't forget

You can edit an individual's entry at any time by clicking on their name and clicking on the Edit button. Click on the Done button once you have finished updating their details.

1 Click on this icon on the Dock, or in the Launchpad

2 Click on an existing contact here

3 Their details are displayed in the right-hand window

4 Click here under the Name panel to add a new contact

5 Enter the person's details

6 Click on the Done button to finish the entry

Adding a Calendar

Electronic calendars are now a standard part of modern life and on the Mac this function is performed by the Calendar app. To create a calendar:

1 Click on this icon on the Dock, or in the Launchpad

2 Select whether to view the calendar by day, week, month or year

3 Click on the Today button to view the current day. Click on the forward or back arrows to move to the next day, week, month or year

To add new events:

1 Select a date and double-click on it, or Ctrl+click on the date and select New Event

2 Enter the details for the new event

3 Double-click on an item and select options for how it is displayed

Don't forget

Calendars and address books can be backed up and shared with the online iCloud service. See Chapter Nine for more details about iCloud.

Don't forget

A quick event can be added to a calendar by clicking on this button at the top of the calendar window and entering the details in the Quick Event box.

Making Notes

It is always useful to have a quick way of making notes of everyday things, such as shopping lists, recipes or packing lists for traveling. With Mountain Lion the Notes app is perfect for this task. To use it:

1 Click on this icon on the Dock, or in the Launchpad

2 The right-hand panel is where the note is created. The left-hand panel displays a list of all notes

3 Click on these buttons to, from left to right, show the folder panel, or the standard view

4 Click on the note area and start typing to create a new note

5 Click on this button to add another note

6 As more notes are added, the most recent appears at the top of the list in the left-hand panel

Sharing Notes

Notes can be shared with other people, or you can use iCloud to make them available on any other iCloud-enabled devices that you have. To share a note:

1 Click on this button at the bottom of a note to email the note or include it in an iMessage to someone

2 To share via iCloud, click on Notes>Accounts... from the Notes menu bar

3 Click on the iCloud button to access the iCloud System Preferences

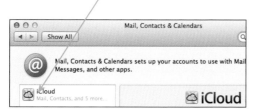

4 Ensure that the box next to Notes is checked On in the iCloud System Preferences. Once this has been done notes will be available on other compatible devices via iCloud

Setting Reminders

Another useful app for keeping organized is Reminders. This enables you to create lists for different topics and then set reminders for specific items. A date and time can be set for each reminder and, when this is reached, the reminder appears on your Mac screen (and in the Notification Center). To use Reminders:

1 Click on this icon on the Dock, or in the Launchpad

2 Lists can be created for different categories of reminders. The Reminder lists are located in the left-hand panel. Click on a list name to add lists here

3 Click on these buttons to, from left to right, show or hide the lists panel, display a calendar for adding reminders on specific dates, or add a new list category

4 Click on this button to add a new reminder, or click on a new line

5 Enter text for the reminder

6 Click on this button to add details for the reminder

7 Check on this button to add a time and date for the reminder

8 Click on the date and select a date for when you want the reminder alert. Do the same for the time, by typing a new time over the existing one

9 If required, add details for a repeat reminder and a priority level

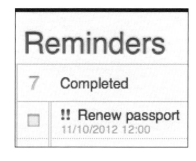

10 Click on the Done button

11 The reminder is set for the specified date and time. This will appear on the screen when the time arrives and also in the Notifications Center, if it is set up for Reminders (see pages 60–61)

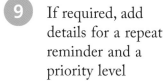

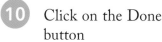

12 Check on this box to move a reminder to the Completed list

Hot tip

For a recurring reminder, click on the Repeat link at Step 9 and select a repeat option from None, Every Day, Every Day, Every Week, Every 2 Weeks, Every Month, Every Year.

Getting Notifications

The Notification Center option provides a single location to view all of your emails, messages, updates and alerts. It appears at the top right-hand corner of the screen. The items that appear in Notifications are set up within System Preferences. To do this:

1 Open System Preferences and click on this icon

2 The items that will appear in the Notification Center are listed here. Click on an item to select it and set its notification options

Don't forget

Twitter feeds and Facebook updates can also be set up to appear in the Notification Center.

3 To disable an item so that is does not appear in the Notification Center, select it as above and check off the Show in Notification Center box

Viewing Notifications

Notifications appear in the Notification Center. The way they appear can be determined in the System Preferences:

1 Select an alert style. A banner alert comes up on the screen and then disappears after a few seconds

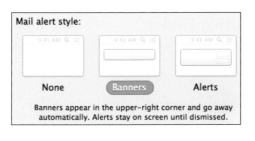

2 The Alerts option shows the notification; it stays on screen until dismissed (such as this one for reminders)

3 Click on this button in the top right-hand corner of the screen to view all of the items in the Notification Center. Click on it again to hide the Notification Center

4 In the Notification Center, click on an item to open it or view more details about it

Hot tip

The Notification Center can also be displayed with a trackpad or Magic Trackpad by dragging with two fingers from right to left, starting from the far right edge.

61

Don't forget

Software updates also appear in the Notification Center, when they are available.

Finding Things

Searching electronic data is now a massive industry, with companies such as Google leading the way with online searching. On Macs it is also possible to search your folders and files, using the built-in search facilities. This can be done either through the Finder or with the Spotlight app.

Using Finder
To search for items within the Finder:

Hot tip

When entering search keywords try to be as specific as possible. This will cut down on the number of unwanted results.

1 In the Finder window, enter the search keyword(s) in this box

2 The results are shown in the Finder window

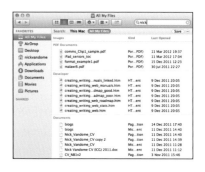

3 Select the areas over which you want the search performed

Don't forget

Both folders and files will be displayed in the Finder as part of the search results.

Search: **This Mac** **All My Files**

4 Double-click on a folder to see its contents

5 Double-click on a file to open it

6 Click once on an item to view its file path on your computer (i.e. where it is actually located)

Using Spotlight

Spotlight is the Mac's dedicated search app. It can be used to search through the files on your Mac. To use Spotlight:

1 Click on this icon at the far right of the Finder Menu bar

2 In the Spotlight box, enter the search keyword(s)

3 The results are displayed according to type

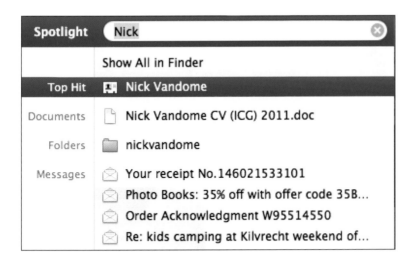

Beware

Spotlight starts searching for items as soon as you start typing a word. So don't worry if some of the first results look inappropriate as these will disappear once you have finished typing the full word.

63

...cont'd

4 Click on an item to view it or see its contents (in the case of folders)

5 If you select a folder, it will be displayed in its location within the Finder

6 Click on the Spotlight Preferences... link

Spotlight Preferences...

7 Order the different content types according to how you would like them displayed in the Spotlight search results

Adding a Printer

OS X Mountain Lion makes the printing process as simple as possible, partly by being able to automatically install new printers as soon as they are connected to your Mac. However, it is also possible to install printers manually. To do this:

1 Open the System Preferences folder and click on the Print & Scan button

2 Click here to add a new printer and click on either the Add Other

Printer or Scanner... link or any available printers

3 OS X Mountain Lion loads the required

printer driver (if it does not have a specific one it will try and use a generic one)

4 The details about the printer are available in the Print & Scan window

Printers

Dell Laser Printer 172...
Idle, Last Used

Dell Laser Printer 1720dn

Open Print Queue...

Options & Supplies...

Location:
Kind: Generic PostScript Printer
Status: Idle

5 Once a printer has been installed documents can be printed by selecting File>Print from the Menu bar. Print settings can be set at this point and they can also be set by selecting File>Page/Print Setup from the Menu bar in most apps

Beware

If you have an old printer your Mac may not identify it and you will have to install the print driver from the disk that came with the printer, or download it from the website of the printer's manufacturer.

External Drives

Attaching external drives is an essential part of mobile computing: whether it is to back up data as you are traveling or for downloading photos and other items. External drives are displayed on the Desktop once they have been attached and they can then be used for the required task. To do this:

1 Attach the external drive. This is usually done with a USB cable. Once it has been attached it is shown on the Desktop

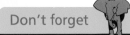
Don't forget

External drives can be items such as pen drives, digital cameras or external hard disks.

2 The drive is shown under the Devices section of the Finder

3 Perform the required task for the external drive (such as copying files or folders onto it from the hard drive of your Mac computer)

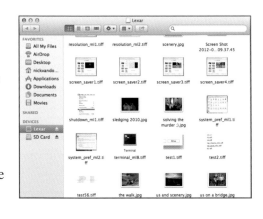

Don't forget

External drives can be renamed by Ctlr+clicking on their name in the Finder and overtyping it with a new name.

4 External drives have to be ejected properly, not just pulled out or removed. To do this, click on this button next to the drive in the Finder window, or drag its icon on the Desktop over the Trash icon on the Dock. This will then change into an Eject icon

4 Leisure Time

Leisure time, and how we use it, is a significant issue for everyone. For Mac users this is recognized with the iLife suite of software. This chapter looks at how to use the apps within iLife to organize and edit photos, play and download music, create your own music and produce and share home movies. It also covers listening to the radio and playing chess.

Downloading Your Photos

For users of digital cameras, iPhoto can be used to download photographs. If you do not have iPhoto, or do not want to use it, any other image-editing app, such as Photoshop Elements, can be used to download digital photographs. But as iPhoto is a dedicated Mac app, this will be used for the following examples.

Photos can be downloaded by connecting your digital camera to your Mac with a USB or Firewire cable. They can also be downloaded with a card reader, into which the camera's memory card can be placed.

Once photographs have been downloaded by iPhoto they are displayed within the Library. This is the storage area for all of the photographs that are added to iPhoto.

From within iPhoto a variety of tasks can be performed. These include organizing, editing and sharing your photographs.

Don't forget

Once a camera has been connected to your Mac, iPhoto will open automatically. Click on the Import button to download the photos from your camera into the iPhoto Library.

Don't forget

iPhoto is part of the iLife suite of apps that covers items such as photos, music, and video. Access it by clicking on this icon on the Dock.

Viewing Photos

There is a variety of ways in which photos can be viewed and displayed in iPhoto.

1 In the main window double-click on an image

2 This displays it at full size (click on it once to return to the main window)

Hot tip

Zooming right in on a photo is an excellent way to view fine detail and see if the photo is properly in focus.

69

3 In the main window drag this slider to display images in the main iPhoto window at different sizes

Slideshows

A popular way of displaying photos is through a slideshow; iPhoto can be used to produce slick and professional-looking shows. To do this:

Hot tip

To select multiple photos, drag around them all, or Ctrl+click on each photo.

1 Select the required images

2 Click on the Slideshow button

3 Select the required settings for the slideshow

4 Click on the Play button

5 Move the cursor over an image and click on this button to access the Settings window

6 The slideshow will run, with the settings specified in Step 3

Creating a Photo Album

One of the first things to do in iPhoto is to create different albums (or folders) for your photographs. This is because the number of photographs will expand quickly and it is important to have different locations for different subject matter. This will make it much easier to organize your photographs and find the ones you want quickly. To create a new album:

1 Under the main panel, click on the Add To button

2 Click on the Album button

3 Click on the New Album button

4 The untitled album appears under the Albums section

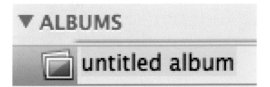

5 Enter a name for the album

...cont'd

6 To add photos to an album, select them from the main window

Don't forget

Once photos have been added to an album they are still visible in the main Library. The items in each album are just a reference back to the Library items.

7 Drag the photos into the album

Beware

If you delete a photo from the Library it will also be deleted from any albums in which it has been placed.

8 Click on an album to view its contents in the main iPhoto window

Enhancing Your Photos

One of the great advantages of digital photos is that they can be edited and enhanced in numerous ways. Although iPhoto is primarily an organizational tool for digital photos, it also serves as a photo editor.

Cropping photos

Cropping involves taking out an area of a photo behind the main subject. To do this:

1 Select a photo

Don't forget

Most photos will benefit from some degree of cropping.

2 Click on the Edit button and click on the Quick Fixes tab

3 Click on the Crop button

4 Drag on the image and drag the corner resizing handles to crop the image

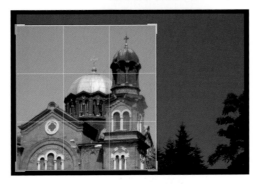

5 Click on the Done button

...cont'd

Color adjustments

To edit the color in a photo:

1 Select a photo

2 Click on the Edit button

3 Click on the Adjust tab

4 Drag the sliders to adjust the various color options in the photo

5 The color adjustments are applied to the selected photo as they are made

6 Click on the Adjust tab again to hide the Adjust window

Removing red-eye

Red-eye can be a common problem when using a flash to take photos of people. However, this can be removed within iPhoto:

1 Select a photo affected by red-eye

2 Click on the Edit button

Don't forget

If you have red-eye in a photo make sure that you always remove it, otherwise it could ruin a perfectly good photo.

3 Click on the Quick Fixes button

4 Click on the Fix Red-Eye button

5 Click on the affected area

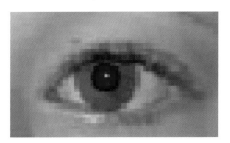

6 The red-eye is removed

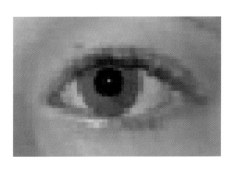

...cont'd

Adding effects

Special effects can be added to photos in iPhoto at the touch of a button. To do this:

1 Select a photo and click on the Edit button

2 Click on the Effects tab

3 Click on one of the available effects

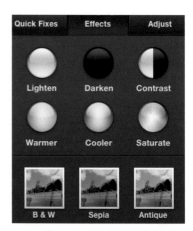

4 The effect is applied to the selected photo

Sharing and Creating

iPhoto offers a number of creative ways in which you can share your photos:

1 Click on the Share button to access options for sharing your photos to popular sharing and social networking sites

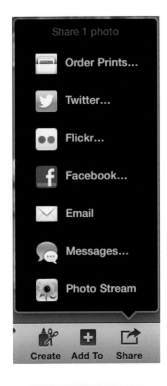

Don't forget

The Order Prints button will automatically connect you to an online printing service appropriate to your current location.

2 Click on the Create button to access options for creating items such as photo books, cards and calendars. These are done with online services

Playing a Music CD

Music is one of the areas that has revived Apple's fortunes in recent years, primarily through the iPod music player and iTunes; and also the iTunes music store, where music can be bought online. iTunes is a versatile app but its basic function is to play a music CD. To do this:

1 Insert the CD in the CD/DVD drive

2 By default, iTunes will open and display this window. Click No if you just want to play the CD

Would you like to import the CD "100 Relaxing Classics [Disc 1]" into your iTunes library?

☐ Do not ask me again

No   Yes

3 Click on the CD name

DEVICES

● 100 Relaxing Classics... ⏏

4 Click on this button to play the whole CD

5 Click on this button if you want to copy the music from the CD onto your hard drive

Import CD

Organizing Your Music

iTunes offers great flexibility when it comes to organizing your music.

① Click here to view all of the music in your iTunes library

② Click on this button to display a quick view of your iTunes music

✓	Name	Time	Artist	▲	Album
✓	Digital Booklet – The Suburbs		Arcade Fire		The Suburbs
✓	The Suburbs	5:15	Arcade Fire		The Suburbs
✓	Ready to Start	4:16	Arcade Fire		The Suburbs
✓	Modern Man	4:40	Arcade Fire		The Suburbs
✓	Rococo	3:57	Arcade Fire		The Suburbs
✓	Empty Room	2:52	Arcade Fire		The Suburbs
✓	City With No Children	3:12	Arcade Fire		The Suburbs
✓	Half Light I	4:14	Arcade Fire		The Suburbs

③ Click on this button to view your iTunes library according to the relevant cover images for the music

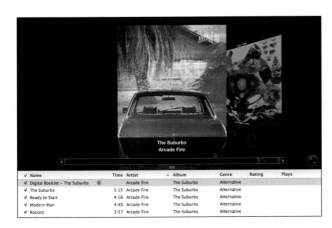

④ Click on this button (Shuffle) to play all of the music in your iTunes library in a random order

...cont'd

Adding a playlist

A playlist in iTunes is a selection of music that you want to group together under certain headings, such as for a party or a certain mood or genre. To create a playlist:

1 Click on this button at the bottom of the Library section panel

2 Enter a name for the new playlist

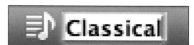

3 Click on the required items of music in the main window

4 Drag the selected items over the playlist folder and release

5 The selected items are included in the playlist

Downloading Music

As well as playing music, iTunes can also be used to legally download music, via the iTunes Store. This contains a huge range of music and you only have to register on the site once. After this you can download music for use on your Mac and also for downloading onto an iPod. To do this:

1 Under the Library section in iTunes, click on the iTunes Store button

2 The iTunes store offers music, videos, television apps, audiobooks and podcasts for downloading

Beware

Never use illegal music download sites. Apart from the legal factor, they are much more likely to contain viruses and spyware.

81

3 Look for items in the iTunes store either by browsing through the sections of the site, or enter a keyword in the search box at the top of the window

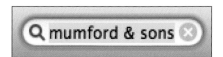

...cont'd

4 Locate an item you want to buy

Don't forget

Once you have registered on iTunes you can then download music from your account to up to five different computers.

5 Click on the Buy button (at this point you will have to register with the iTunes Store, if you have not already done so)

Buy Album

6 Once you have registered, you will have to enter a username and password to complete your purchase

7 Once the item has been downloaded it is available through iTunes on your Mac, under the Purchased button

Adding an iPod

Since their introduction in 2001 iPods have become an inescapable part of modern life. It is impossible to sit on a bus or a train without seeing someone with the ubiquitous white earbuds, humming away to their favorite tunes. iPods are for everyone and they should not be seen as solely for the young – although they may select a slightly different type of music to play on them. iPods are designed to work seamlessly with iTunes and the latter can be used to load music onto the former. To do this:

Don't forget

iPods come in a variety of styles, colors and disk capacity.

1. Connect your iPod to the Mac with the supplied USB or Firewire cable

2. iTunes will open automatically and display details about the attached iPod

3. iTunes will automatically start copying music from the iTunes Library onto the iPod. If not, select the iPod under the Devices heading

4. Select File>Sync from the iTunes Menu bar to synchronize iTunes and your iPod

Beware

If you do not want iTunes to sync with your iPod automatically, this can be done manually instead. To do this, select iTunes>Preferences from the Menu bar. Click on the Devices tab and check on the box next to 'Prevent iPods, iPhones and iPads from syncing automatically'. After this you can add content to the iPod by dragging it from the iTunes window to the iPod name in the iTunes sidebar.

Earbuds and Headphones

When listening to music there will probably be occasions when you will want to use either earbuds or headphones to save other people from hearing your music. The choice between the two could have a significant impact on your overall audio experience and comfort.

Earbuds

These are essentially small plastic buds that fit inside the ear. The most common example is the earbuds supplied with iPods. While these are small and convenient, they do not usually offer the best sound quality and, perhaps more importantly for some people, they can be uncomfortable to use, particularly for prolonged periods.

Headphones

These go over the ears rather than in them and are generally more comfortable as a result. It is worth investing in a good set of headphones because the sound quality will ensure that it is money well spent. The one downside of headphones is that they can be slightly bulky, but some are designed so that they fold away into a small, compact pouch.

Creating Music

For those who are as interested in creating music as listening to it, GarageBand can be used for this very purpose. It can take a bit of time and practice to become fully proficient with GarageBand but it is worth persevering with if you are musically inclined and want to compose your own. To use GarageBand:

1 Click on this icon on the Dock

2 Click on the New Project button

3 Give your new project a name and select a instrument with which to create it

Piano

85

4 Click on this button to start recording

5 Click on the keyboard to record the music

Keyboard – Grand Piano

...cont'd

6 Click on this button to view a library of music loops which can be included in your song

7 A list of pre-recorded music loops is displayed

When you open GarageBand, the keyboard for music creation is already open and visible.

8 Select a style and an instrument. The available loops are displayed underneath the Name tab

9 Select a loop and drag it onto the timeline to add it to your song

10 The completed song is shown in the timeline. This can consist of several separate tracks

Listening to the Radio

For the radio lover, iTunes offers literally hundreds of digital radio stations. To access these:

1 Under the Library section in iTunes, click on the Radio button

2 Select a category

Beware

Most major commercial radio stations are not available through the iTunes radio feature. However, there are many apps, for example TuneIn Radio, which allow you to listen to radio stations worldwide.

3 Select a station from the required category. Double-click on it to access the station

4 The station currently playing is shown at the top of the iTunes window

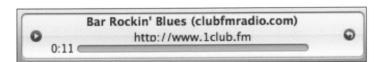

Creating a Home Movie

For home movie buffs, iMovie offers options for downloading, editing and publishing your efforts:

1 Click on this button on the Dock

2 Attach a digital video camera to your Mac with a Firewire cable

3 Click here to access the camera

4 Click here to play the video in the camera

5 Click on the Capture button to copy the video into iMovie

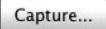

6 Click on the Done button to return to the editing environment

7 Downloaded video clips are shown here

New Event 25-08-2011

8 Drag a clip into the Project Library window to add it to a new video project

Project Library

Don't forget

Video clips can be edited by selecting them in the project window and then clicking on the Clip Trimmer option at the bottom left of the clip. The clip can then be trimmed by dragging the beginning or the end of the clip.

9   Click on this button to access Transition options

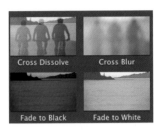

10   Click on this button to access Text options

11   Click on this button to access Sound options

12   Text, transitions and sound can be added to a movie by dragging them between the video clips

13   Click Share on the Menu bar and select an option for exporting the finished movie

Beware

Downloaded video can take up a lot of space on your hard drive.

Sharing a Home Movie

Once video has been created, it can be shared between family and friends on a DVD. This can be done through the iDVD app. To do this:

1 Click on this icon on the Dock

2 Click on the Create a New Project option

3 Give the project a name

4 Click on the Create button

5 Click on the Themes button

6 Double-click on a theme to select it as the background of your DVD

7 Click on the Media button

Media

8 Click on the Photos tab

Photos

9 Select a photo and drag it onto the Drop Zones of the theme

Don't forget

If Drop Zones are left empty a warning will appear when you try and burn the final DVD. However, this can be ignored.

10 Click on the Movies tab

Movies

11 Select a movie and drag it onto the Theme

...cont'd

12 Click on the movie name and type a new name if required

13 Click on the Audio tab

Audio

14 Select an audio element that you want to use as background music for the DVD and drag it onto the Theme

Audio	Photos	Movies

▶ 🎸 GarageBand

▼ 🎵 iTunes

  🎵 Music

  🎞 Movies

  🎙 Podcasts

  📖 Books

  🎵 Purchased

Name	Artist	Time
🎵 The Suburbs	Arcade Fire	5:15
🎵 Ready to Start	Arcade Fire	4:15
🎵 Modern Man	Arcade Fire	4:39
🎵 Rococo	Arcade Fire	3:56
🎵 Empty Room	Arcade Fire	2:51
🎵 City With No Children	Arcade Fire	3:11

15 Click on this button to edit the Drop Zone

16 Click on this button to view the animation of the Theme

17 Click on this button to preview the project

Hot tip

Burn DVDs at a slower speed than the maximum available. This will ensure a better chance of it being burned correctly.

18 Click on this button to burn the finished DVD

Playing Chess

Game playing relaxation is not ignored on the Mac and many hours can be spent playing chess against the computer. To do this:

1 In Finder, click on the Applications button or access the Launchpad

2 Double-click on the Chess icon

3 By default you are white and the computer is black

4 Move your pieces by clicking on them and dragging them to the required square

5 Once you have moved, Black will move automatically

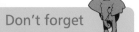

Don't forget

In the Chess application it is possible to play against the computer or another person. This can be specified when you select Game>New to start a new game.

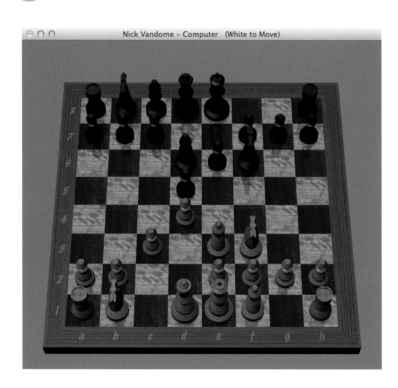

5 At Home

This chapter reveals options for getting productive and creative on your Mac, creating letters, household budgets and presentations.

Productivity Options

As well as using Macs for leisure and entertainment activities, they are also ideally suited for more functional purposes such as creating letters and documents, doing household expenses and creating posters or presentations. As always in the world of technology there is more than one option for which app to use when performing these tasks. Some of these include:

iWork

This is an Apple app that is designed specifically for the Mac. It contains a suite of productivity apps including those for word processing, spreadsheets and presentations. Although not as well known as the more ubiquitous Microsoft Office suite of apps, iWork is an easy-to-use and powerful option that will fulfil the productivity needs of most users. The iWork apps are Pages, Numbers and Keynote and they can all be bought from the App Store.

Where applicable, the productivity examples in this chapter use iWork.

Microsoft Office

Even in the world of Macs it is impossible to avoid the software giant that is Microsoft. For users of Microsoft Office (the suite of apps containing the likes of Word, Excel, Powerpoint) the good news is that there is a version written specifically for the Mac. This works in the same way as the IBM-compatible PC version and for anyone who has used it before the Mac version will look reassuringly familiar. However, on the downside, Office is relatively expensive and the apps contain a lot of functionality that most users will never need.

TextEdit

For anyone who just wants to do some fairly basic word processing, the built-in Mac app TextEdit is an option. This can be used to create letters and other similar documents. However, it does not have the versatility of either iWork or Microsoft Office.

Hot tip

Files in both iWork and Microsoft Office for the Mac can easily be saved for use elsewhere on a Windows PC.
To do this, select the required file format in the Save window.

Accessing a Dictionary

A dictionary is a good starting point for any productivity function. On the Mac you do not have to worry about having a large book to hand as there are two options that cover this task.

Applications dictionary

Within the Applications folder there is a fully-functioning dictionary. To use this:

1 In Finder, click on the Applications button or access the Launchpad

2 Double-click on the Dictionary icon

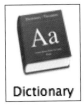

Dictionary

3 Select the option you want to use for looking up a word

4 In the search box, type in the word you want to look up

5 The results are displayed in the dictionary window

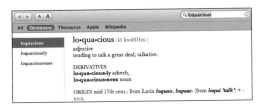

...cont'd

Dashboard dictionary

The Dashboard is an app within Mac OS X that offers a number of widgets, or small apps, for a variety of useful tasks such as weather reports, maps, a clock and a calculator. It also has a dictionary. To use this:

1 Click on this icon on the Dock to access the Dashboard widgets

2 If the Dictionary widget is not showing click on this button to view the available widgets

3 Click on the Dictionary widget to add it to the main Dashboard (which appears above the Desktop)

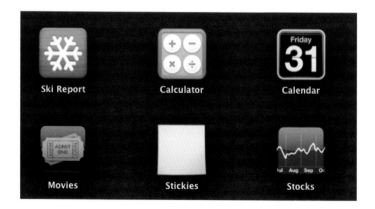

4 The Dictionary widget can be used in a similar way to the one on the previous page

Creating a Letter

One of the most common word processing tasks is writing a letter and it is something that most of us have to do for either business or pleasure. This could be a letter to a family member or a letter of complaint. Whatever the subject matter it is worth making your letters look as professional, or as stylish, as possible. To create a letter in Pages:

1 In Finder, click on the Applications button or access the Launchpad

2 Click on the Pages icon and select File>New from Template Chooser

3 Click on the Letters option

Don't forget

There are enough different letter templates in Pages for you not to need to create your own. If required, existing ones can be amended.

4 Click on a style for the type of letter you want to create

5 Click on the Choose button

...cont'd

6 An untitled letter is displayed based on the template you have selected

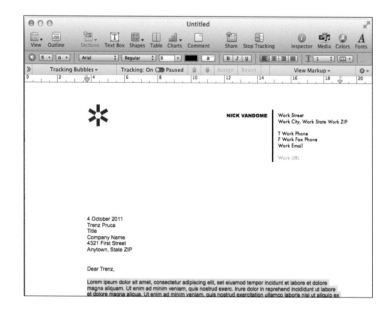

7 Double-click on an element of the letter and overtype to change it

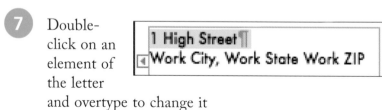

8 Click once in the draft text of the letter. This will highlight all of the text

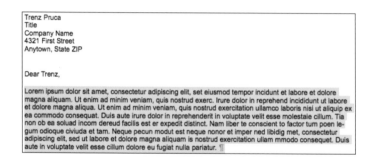

9 Write your own text for the letter

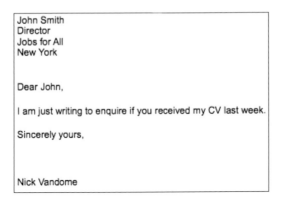

```
John Smith
Director
Jobs for All
New York


Dear John,

I am just writing to enquire if you received my CV last week.

Sincerely yours,



Nick Vandome
```

10 Select File>Save... from the Menu bar

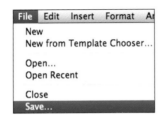

11 Browse to the folder into which you want to save the letter

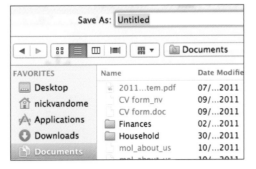

12 Give the letter a name

Save As: work_enquiry

13 Click on the Save button

Save

Formatting a Newsletter

Newsletters are not just the preserve of the business world; they are a great source of information for local clubs, communities and also for family updates. To create and format a newsletter in Pages:

1 In Finder, click on the Applications button or access the Launchpad

2 Click on the Pages icon

3 In the Template Chooser window, click on the Newsletters option

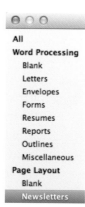

4 Click on a style for the type of newsletter you want to create

5 Click on the Choose button

6 Click on a text element to select it

the SMITH *family*

7 Overtype the selection with your own text

the VANDOMES

When an element is selected it is highlighted by a box with small markers around its perimeter. By dragging these markers you can resize the item.

103

8 Click on an image placeholder (this is just a default image that can be changed with your own photos)

9 Click on the Media button on the toolbar

Media

...cont'd

10 In the Media window browse to the photo you want to use

Don't forget

The Media browser is a quick way to access your iPhoto Library. However, photos have to have been imported into iPhoto for them to be visible in the Media browser.

11 Drag the selected photo onto the placeholder

12 If required, you can drag the image around the page to re-position it

13 Click on the Pages button on the toolbar to add new pages to the newsletter

Pages

14 Click on the type of new page you want to include

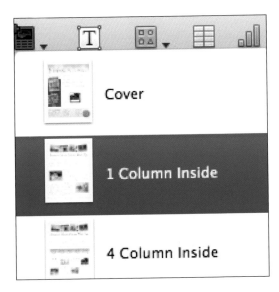

15 Format the new page in the same way as the cover page

Vandome Family Vacation

16 Save the newsletter in the same way as a letter

Using a Calculator

Financial matters can sometimes be a chore but they are a necessary part of life, whether it is working out household expenses or calculating available spending money. Even for the best mathematicians a calculator is a trusty friend when it comes to arithmetic. Luckily the Mac has one ready-made:

1 In Finder, click on the Applications button or access the Launchpad

2 Double-click on the Calculator icon

3 Click on the calculator's buttons to perform calculations

Don't forget

If you are going to be doing anything more than basic calculations, the scientific option may be more useful than the basic one.

4 Select View from the Menu bar and select an option for the type of calculator being displayed

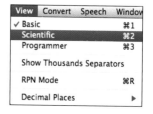

5 The option selected in Step 4 is now available

Doing Household Accounts

As well as being useful for word processing iWork can also be used for financial accounting, such as keeping track of the household accounts. To do this:

1 In Finder, click on the Applications button or access the Launchpad

2 Double-click on the Numbers icon

3 Select File>New from Template Chooser

4 In the template window click on the Personal Finance button

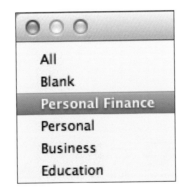

Don't forget

Although any type of accounts are a chore, the more they are kept up to date the easier it is to control them.

5 Select the Budget template

6 Click on the Choose button

Choose

...cont'd

7 The budget template is displayed. All of the items can be

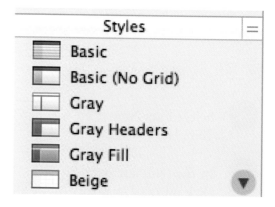

Monthly Net Income			Additional Income		
Income Type	Amount		Details	Month	Amount
Monthly Net Income	£4,500		Mid Year Bonus	June	£2,000
Other Monthly Income	£2,500		Year End Bonus	December	£3,000
				January	
Available Cash	£7,000		Total Additional Income		£5,000

Monthly Expenses			Planned Expenses		
Expense	Costs		Expenditure	Month	Amount
Mortgage	£2,300		November vacation	November	£450
Taxes	£600		Home for the holidays	December	£600
Car Payment	£350		Gifts for family	December	£300
Car Insurance	£60		Family vacation	July	£880
Home Owners Insurance	£127			January	
Cable Bill	£120			January	
Gas/Electric	£88			January	
Monthly Prescription	£50			January	
Total Monthly Expenses	£3,695		Total Planned Expenses		£2,230

edited with your own information

8 Click on a style to change the formatting of the displayed budget

Styles

- Basic
- Basic (No Grid)
- Gray
- Gray Headers
- Gray Fill
- Beige

9 Click on one of the budget topics

10 The selected element is highlighted

Monthly Expenses

Expense	Costs
Mortgage	£2,300
Taxes	£600
Car Payment	£350
Car Insurance	£60
Home Owners Insurance	£127
Cable Bill	£120
Gas/Electric	£88
Monthly Prescription	£50
Total Monthly Expenses	£3,695

11 Double-click on an individual item to select it

4 **Car Payment**

12 Overtype the selected item with your own details

4 **Motor Home Payment**

13 Select a cell containing financial information. Edit the information, as required

£120

£88

£50

£3,695

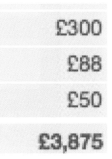

Don't forget

Linked cells are controlled by a mathematical equation that ensures that if one is updated then the data in the linked cell changes too.

14 Linked cells are updated accordingly

£300

£88

£50

£3,875

15 Save the spreadsheet in the same way as for a letter or a newsletter

Creating a Presentation

Presentations are a great way to produce customized slideshows of family photographs or promote activities in local clubs or charities. To do this in iWork:

1   In Finder, click on the Applications button or access the Launchpad

2   Click on the Keynote icon

Don't forget

Keynote is the iWork equivalent of Microsoft Powerpoint.

3   Select File>New from Template Chooser

4   Click on a type of presentation

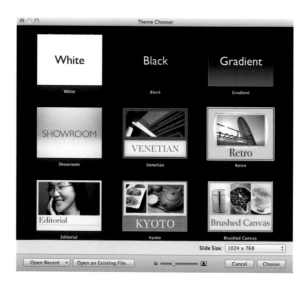

5   Click on the Choose button

6 Double-click on the text to select it

My Slideshow

Double-click to edit

7 Overtype with your own text

8 Click on the Media button on the Menu bar

9 Browse to your photos

111

10 Drag a selected photo onto the placeholder photo on the slide. This replaces the placeholder photo with your own

...cont'd

11 To add more text to a slide, click on the Text Box button on the Menu bar

12 Drag the text tool on the slide to create a text box and type the required text

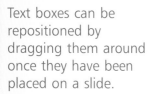
112

13 Click on these buttons for options for formatting the color and type of the text

14 To add more slides click on the New button on the Menu bar. Add content in the same way as the original slide

15 Click on the Play button on the Menu bar to preview the presentation

16 Save the presentation in the same way as a letter, a newsletter or a spreadsheet

6 Getting Online

Accessing the Internet and World Wide Web (WWW) is essential for most computer users. This chapter shows you how to use your Mac to start browsing the web with the web browser Safari.

Accessing the Internet

Access to the Internet is an accepted part of the computing world and it is unusual for users not to want to do this. Not only does this provide a gateway to the World Wide Web but also email.

Connecting to the Internet with a Mac is done through the System Preferences. To do this:

1 Click on the System Preferences icon on the Dock

2 Click on the Network icon

3 Check that your method of connecting to the Internet is active, i.e. colored green

4 Click on the Assist Me... button to access wizards for connecting to the Internet with your preferred method of connection

Around the Web

When you are surfing the web it is important to feel comfortable with both your browser and also the websites at which you are looking. Most websites are a collection of linked pages that you can move between by clicking on links (also known as hyperlinks) that connect the different pages.

Address bar

The Address bar is the box at the top of the browser that displays the address of the web page that is currently being displayed. Each web page has a unique address so the address changes whenever you move to a different page. The Address bar displays the web page address in this format:

Main content

The full content of a web page is displayed in the main browser window:

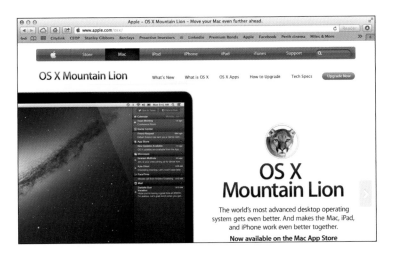

Macs have a built-in web browser known as Safari. This can be accessed from the Dock by clicking on this icon:

...cont'd

Toolbar

This is a collection of icons at the top of the browser that has various options for navigating around web pages and accessing options such as newsfeeds and printing pages:

Menu bar

This contains various menus with options for navigating around, and customizing web pages. In Safari it is located at the top of the Safari window:

Safari   File   Edit   View   History   Bookmarks   Window   Help

Navigation bars

These are groups of buttons that appear on websites to help users navigate within the site. Generally, the main navigation bars appear in the same place on every page of the site:

Home   Books by Category »   Bookstore   News   About In Easy Steps »

Search box

Most websites have a search box, into which keywords or phrases can be entered to search over the whole site:

Vandome

Hot tip

The Toolbar contains a homepage button which takes you to your own homepage, i.e. the page that is accessed when you first open up your browser.

Don't forget

The items that make up the navigation bar are buttons, or textual links, that take you to another location within the site.

Links

This is the device that is used to move between pages within a website, or from one website to another. Links can be in a variety of styles, but most frequently they are in the form of buttons, underlined text or a roll-over (i.e. a button or piece of text that changes appearance when the cursor is passed over it):

terms of use : privacy policy : write for us : accessibility

Don't forget

The cursor usually turns into a pointing hand when it is passed over a link on a website.

Tabs

Safari has an option for using different tabs. This enables you to open different web pages within the same browser window. You can then move between the pages by clicking on each tab, at the top of the window. They can also be minimized so that you can swipe through available tabs:

Bookmarks

Everyone has their favorite web pages that they return to again and again. These can be added to a list in a browser so that they can be accessed quickly when required. There is usually a button at the top of the browser that can add the current page to the list of bookmarked items:

History	Bookmarks	Window	Help

Setting a Homepage

A homepage is what a browser opens by default whenever it is first launched. This is usually a page associated with the company that created the browser, i.e. the Apple homepage for Safari. However, it is possible to customize the browser so that it opens with your own choice of homepage. To do this in Safari:

Don't forget

A unique web page address is known as a URL. This stands for Uniform Resource Locator and means that every page on the web is unique.

1 Open Safari and click on Safari>Preferences... from the Menu bar

Safari	File	Edit	View
About Safari			
Safari Extensions...			
Report Bugs to Apple...			
Preferences...			

2 Click on the General tab

3 Click on the Set to Current Page if you want the current page you are viewing to be your homepage

Set to Current Page

4 Enter a web address in the Homepage box to set this as your homepage

Homepage: http://www.apple.com/

5 Click on this button to close the Preferences window

About Safari

Safari is a web browser that is designed specifically to be used with OS X. It is similar in most respects to other browsers, but it usually functions more quickly and works seamlessly with OS X.

Safari overview

1 Click here on the Dock to launch Safari

2 All of the controls are at the top of the browser

Toolbar   Address/Search bar   Reader tabs

Bookmarks bar and buttons

Hot tip

If the Bookmarks bar is not visible, select View from the Menu bar and check on the Show Bookmarks bar option. From this menu you can also select or deselect items such as showing All Tabs, the Status bar and the Reading list.

119

Smart Search box

One of the innovations in the latest version of Safari (6) is that the Address bar and the Search box have been incorporated into one. You can use the same box for searching, or enter a web address to go to that page.

Don't forget

The button next to the Reader button is the Download button. This shows items that you have downloaded from websites with Safari.

1 Click in the box to enter an item

2 Results are presented as web pages or search results.

Click on the appropriate item to go to it, i.e. directly to a website or to the search results page

Safari Tabbed Browsing

Tabs are now a familiar feature on web browsers, so you can have multiple sites open within the same browser window.

1 When more than one tab is open, the tabs appear at the top of the web pages

Apple   In Easy Steps bookshop – the home of sm...   +   ▥

2 Click on this button next to the tabs to open a new tab

3 Click on one of the Top Sites (see page 121) or enter a website address in the Address Bar

4 Click on this button next to the new tab button to minimize all of the current tabs

5 Move left and right to view all of the open tabs in thumbnail view. Click on one to view it at full size

Don't forget

Safari is a full-screen app and can be expanded by clicking the double arrow in the top right corner. For more information on full-screen apps, see Chapter Two.

Safari Top Sites

Within Safari there is a facility to view a graphical representation of the websites that you visit most frequently. This can be done from a button on the Safari Menu bar. To do this:

1 Click on this button to view the Top Sites window

2 The Top Sites window contains thumbnails of the websites that you have visited most frequently with Safari (this builds up as you visit more sites)

3 Click on the Edit button to change the properties of the Top Sites thumbnails

4 Click on the cross to delete a thumbnail from the Top Sites window. Click on the pin to keep it there permanently

5 Click on a thumbnail to go to the full site

6 Use these buttons to select the size of the thumbnails

7 To add a new site to the Top Sites, open another window and drag the URL (website address) into the Top Sites

Don't forget

The Top Sites window is also accessed if you open a new tab within Safari.

Adding Bookmarks

Bookmarks allow you to create quick links to your favorite web pages or the ones you visit most frequently. Bookmarks can be added to a menu or the Bookmarks bar in Safari, which makes them even quicker to access. Folders can also be created to store the less-frequently used bookmarks. To view and create bookmarks:

1 Click here to view all bookmarks

2 All of the saved bookmarks can be accessed from the Collections panel and viewed in the main window. Click on a page to move to it

3 Click here to create a bookmark for the page currently being viewed

4 Enter a name for the bookmark and select a location in which to store it

5 Click on the Add button

Viewing Your Online History

In any web session it is possible to look at dozens, or hundreds, of websites and pages. To make it easier to retrace your steps and return to previously-viewed pages, the History option in Safari can be used. To do this:

1 Select History from the Safari Menu bar

2 Click on an item here to return to a page that has been viewed in your current browsing session

3 Click on a date to view items that have been accessed previously

Saturday, 4 August 2012
Friday, 3 August 2012
Thursday, 2 August 2012
Wednesday, 1 August 2012

4 Click on Clear History to remove all of the items in your browsing history

Monday, 30 July 2012

Clear History...

Hot tip

To avoid your browsing history being recorded, select Safari>Private Browsing from the menu bar. This will mean that nothing is recorded from your browsing session.

123

Beware

If you clear your browsing history your browser will not remember any address that you have previously entered. If the history is not cleared, the browser will remember them as soon as you start typing the address.

Safari Reader

Web pages can be complex and cluttered things at times. On occasions you may want to just read the content of one story on a web page without all of the extra material in view. In Safari this can be done with the Reader function. To do this:

1 Select View>Show Reader from the Safari menu bar

2 Click on the Reader button in the address bar of a web page that supports this functionality

3 The button turns a slightly darker blue once the Reader is activated

4 The content is displayed in a text format, with any photos from the original

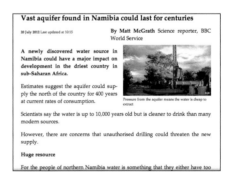

5 Click on this button on the Safari toolbar if you want to save a page to read at a later date

6 Click on this button to add the page

Add Page

7 Being Interactive Online

This chapter shows some of the activities that can be undertaken on the web. It covers buying items from online shops, delving into your family history and playing online games.

Shopping Online

The web is a lot more than just a means of discovering facts and figures. It is also a means of doing business in terms of buying and selling. This can be for small or large purchases, but either way, online shopping has revolutionized our retail lives.

When you are shopping online there are some guidelines that should be followed to try to ensure you are in a safe online environment and do not spend too much money:

- Make a note of what you want to buy and stick to this once you have found it. Online shopping sites are adept at displaying a lot of enticing offers and it is a lot easier to buy something by clicking a button than it is to physically take it to a checkout

- Never buy anything that is promoted to you via an email, unless it is from a company who you have asked to send you promotional information

- When paying for items, make sure that the online site has a secure area for accepting payment and credit card details. A lot of sites display information about this within their payment area and another way to ascertain this is to check in the Address bar of the payment page. If it is within a secure area the address of the page will start with "https" rather than the standard "http"

Using online shopping

The majority of online shopping sites are similar in their operation:

- Goods are identified

- Goods are placed in a shopping basket

- Once the shopping is completed you proceed to the checkout

- You enter your shipping details and pay for the goods, usually with a credit or debit card

On some sites you have to register before you can buy goods and in some cases this enables you to perform your shopping quicker by using a 1-click system. This means that all of your billing and payment details are already stored on the site and you can buy goods simply by clicking one button without having to re-enter your details. One of the most prominent sites to use this method is Amazon:

Beware

Be careful when shopping online as you can quickly get carried away since making purchases can be so easy.

127

Booking a Vacation

Just as many retailers have been creating an online presence, the same is also true for vacation companies and travel agents. It is now possible to book almost any type of vacation on the web, from cruises to city breaks.

Several sites offer full travel services where they can deal with flights, hotels, insurance, car hire and excursions. These sites include:

- www.expedia.com

- www.travelocity.com

- www.tripadvisor.com

These sites usually list special offers and last-minute deals on their homepages and there is also a facility for specifying your precise requirements. To do this:

1 Select your vacation requirements

2 Enter flight details (if applicable)

3 Enter dates for your vacation

4 Click on the Search button

In addition to sites that do everything for you it is also possible to book your vacation on individual sites. This can be particularly useful for cruises and also for booking hotels around the world. Some websites to look at are:

Cruises

- www.cruises.com
- www.carnival.com
- www.princess.com

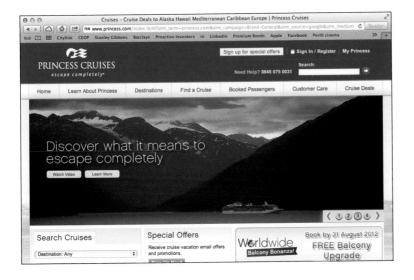

Don't forget

Vacation and hotel websites usually have versions that are specific to the geographical location in which you are situated.

129

Hotels

- www.hotels.com
- www.laterooms.com
- www.choicehotels.com

Researching Family History

A recent growth industry on the web has been family history, or genealogy. Hundreds of organizations around the world have now digitized their records concerning individuals and family histories and there are numerous websites that provide online access to these records. Some of these sites are:

- www.ancestry.com

- www.genealogy.com

- www.familysearch.org

- www.rootsweb.com

130

Most genealogy sites require you to register, for a fee, before you can conduct extensive family research on their sites, but once you do the process is similar on them all:

1 Enter the details of the family members in the search boxes

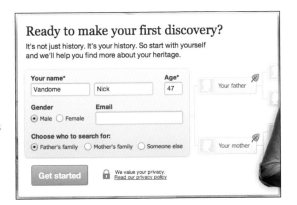

2 Click on the Get started button

3 The results are displayed for the names searched

Don't forget

Some sites offer a free initial search, but after that you will have to pay for each search.

131

4 Click on the Search for Records button to get a detailed report for your information. This may require registering on the site

5 On some sites there is a facility for creating your family tree. Enter the relevant details

Price Comparison Sites

Everyone likes to get value for money when shopping or, better still, a bargain. On the web it is possible to try to find the best possible prices for items before you buy them. This is done through price comparison sites that show the prices for items from a range of online retailers. Some of the price comparison sites include:

- www.pricegrabber.com

- www.pricerunner.com

- www.pricewatch.com

To use a price comparison site:

Don't forget

Price comparison sites do not actually sell anything: they just direct you to different retailers.

1 Select one of the online price comparison sites

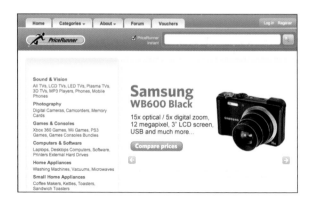

2 Select a category for the type of product you want to buy

> **Sound & Vision**
> All TVs, LCD TVs, LED TVs, Plasma TVs, 3D TVs, MP3 Players, Phones, Mobile Phones

3 Locate the product you want to buy

4 Click on the Compare Prices link or tab

Compare prices

5 The available retailers and their prices are displayed

Retailer	Rating	Retailer message	Price	Availability
1staudiovisual Info on 1st Audio Visual	★★★★★ 2 reviews	**SAMSUNG UE46D7000 46" FULL HD 3D LED TV PLUS FREE GALAXY S** free samsung galaxy s tablet wi-fi 5.0 8gb yp-g70cw	£ 1,394.95 + Shipping : £ 0.00 **£ 1,394.95**	🛍 In stock 04/10/11 **Go to store**
AJ ELECTRONICS Info on AJ Electronics	★★★★★ 1773 reviews ⊘ CUSTOMER CERTIFIED	**SAMSUNG UE46D7000 46In FHD SLIM SMART 3D LED TV** Only UK Original Goods and Full UK Warranty. London Showroom. FREE DELIVERY ON ALL PRODUCTS. Family Run Company. Est. Since 1983.	£ 1,395.00 + Shipping : £ 0.00 **£ 1,395.00**	🛍 In stock 1 - 2 days 04/10/11 **Go to store**

6 Click on a retailer's link or icon to go to its site, from where the item can be purchased

Shopping on eBay

eBay is one of the phenomena of the online world. Started as a small site in California it has grown into a multi-billion dollar business with online auctions and also standard online retailer transactions. To buy and sell items on eBay you have to be registered. This can be done from the eBay homepage by clicking on the Register button or link. This takes you through the registration process, which is free.

Buying items

Once you have registered you can start buying and selling items. In some ways it is better to start by buying some cheaper items just to get used to the system. To do this:

Beware

Most people are honest on eBay but you do sometimes get unscrupulous buyers and sellers, so be sure to view a seller's feedback before you commit to buying anything.

1 To find items to buy, enter a keyword in the search box and click on the Search button, or

stamps

Search

2 Click on the Categories button and drill down through the various categories

✓ All Categories
Antiques
Art
Baby
Books
Business & Industrial
Cameras & Photo
Cars, Boats, Vehicles & Parts
Cell Phones & PDAs
Clothing, Shoes & Accessories
Coins & Paper Money
Collectibles
Computers & Networking
Consumer Electronics
Crafts
Dolls & Bears
DVDs & Movies

3 When you find items in which you are interested, select whether you want to view them according to Auctions, Buy It Now (single price purchase) or both

All items   Auctions only   Buy It Now

4 Click on an item to view its details

TRAINS Locomotives ST VINCENT MNH Progressive Proofs 90...
Returns: Accepted within 7 days

5 For Buy It Now items, click on this button to purchase the item

6 For auction items, enter a bid in the Place Bid box and click on the Place Bid button

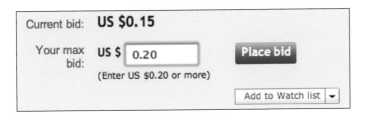

Current bid: **US $0.15**

Your max bid: **US $** 0.20   **Place bid**

(Enter US $0.20 or more)

Add to Watch list ▾

7 Review the item and purchase details

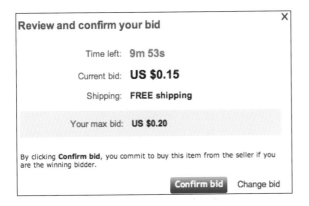

Review and confirm your bid   ✕

Time left: **9m 53s**

Current bid: **US $0.15**

Shipping: **FREE shipping**

Your max bid: **US $0.20**

By clicking **Confirm bid**, you commit to buy this item from the seller if you are the winning bidder.

Confirm bid   Change bid

Don't forget

Once you have completed the transaction you can leave feedback about the seller.

8 If you want to proceed with your bid, click on the Confirm bid button

Confirm bid

9 If you are successful in the auction you will be notified on eBay and also via email. At this point you pay the vendor for the item and they should mail it to you

...cont'd

Selling items

If you want to sell items on eBay you have to first list them for sale. To do this:

1 Click on the Sell button at the top of the eBay window

2 Click on the List your item button

List your item

3 Enter the keywords for your item and click on the Start selling button

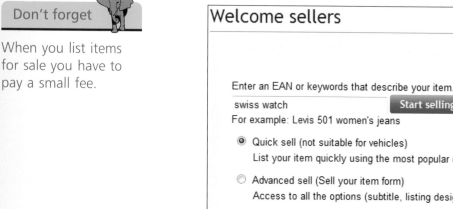

4 Complete the wizard for selling items. This includes a detailed description of the item and photographs

5 Once the wizard has been completed the item will be listed in the relevant category on eBay

Online Finances

Online banking

Online banking has helped to transform our financial activities in the same way as online shopping has transformed our retail ones. Most major banks have online banking facilities and they can be used for a number of services, including:

- Managing your accounts
- Transferring money
- Paying bills
- Applying for credit cards
- Paying credit cards
- Applying for loans

Before you can use any of these online services you have to first register and apply for an online account:

Don't forget

Online banking is generally as secure as any other form of banking transaction and it has the advantage that you can check your accounts as frequently as you like.

1 On the homepage of most bank websites there are boxes for signing in if you are an existing online customer or applying for a new account. Select the relevant option and you will then be taken through the necessary steps

...cont'd

Stocks and shares online

An extension of online banking is being able to deal in stocks and shares on the web. You can buy and sell on the stock market without having to leave the comfort of your own home. A number of financial services websites offer this facility and they also provide a lot of background information as well as the buying and selling function. If you are going to be trading stocks and shares on the web it is a good idea to find out as much about them before you start trading. In this respect the websites of relevant stock markets provide a very useful source of information:

Beware

Never buy stocks and shares from any offers you receive by email.

1   Enter details to get current stock prices

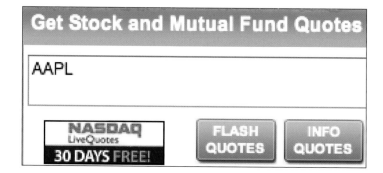

2   Use the Research areas to find out the history and performance of individual stocks and shares

Quotes & Research

3   Check the latest News section for updates

News & Commentary

Maps Online

Maps have fascinated mankind for thousands of years and with the web it has never been easier to view local, national or international maps. In addition, the sites that provide these services also provide a host of additional information about hotels, airports, schools and civic amenities. Two sites to look at for maps are:

- www. multimap.com

- http://maps.google.com

To use an online mapping service:

Don't forget

Multimap now appears under the Bing website, but it can still be accessed with the Multimap address.

1 Enter a name or zip code of somewhere you want to look up

Colorado, United States

2 The results display the required map

Don't forget

Mac devices also have their own Map app.

3 Use this slider to zoom in or out of the map

Online Games

Online gambling has developed in some countries in recent years but it is also possible to play online games, such as bridge and backgammon, without the need to gamble away your life savings. Although some of these sites do allow you to play for money, others offer a less financially pressurized environment. For both bridge and backgammon sites you can either play against the computer or other people who are on the site. Either way, you are usually presented with a graphic interface of the action:

Don't forget

Sites for online bridge or backgammon can be found by entering these keywords into the Google search box.

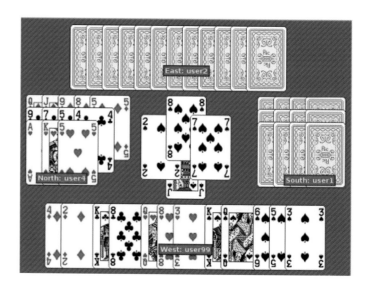

Don't forget

The Game Center app can also be used for downloading games from the App Store.

Game Center

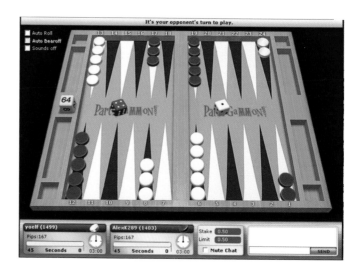

8 Keeping in Touch

Communication, as much as money, makes the world go round. This chapter shows how to use the Mac tools to communicate, interact and share by email, text and video.

Setting up Email

Email is an essential element for most computer users and Macs come with their own email app called Mail. This covers all of the email functionality that anyone could need.

When first using Mail you have to set up your email account. This information will be available from the company who provides your email service, although in some cases Mail may obtain this information automatically. To view your Mail account details:

1 Click on this icon on the Dock

2 Select Mail>Preferences... from the Menu bar

3 Click on the Accounts tab

4 If it has not already been included, enter the details of your email account in the Account Information section

5 Click on this button to close the Mail Preferences window

Adding Mailboxes

Before you start creating email messages it is a good idea to create a folder structure (mailboxes) for your emails. This will allow you to sort your emails into relevant subjects when you receive them, rather than having all of them sitting in your Inbox. To add new mailboxes:

1 Mailboxes are displayed in the Mailboxes panel

2 At the bottom of the Mailboxes panel, click on this icon

3 Select where you want the mailbox to be created (by default this will be On My Mac)

4 Enter a name for the new mailbox

5 Click on the OK button

6 The new mailbox is added to the current list

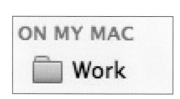

Don't forget

Different mailboxes can be used to store emails according to their subject matter.

Creating Email

Mail enables you to send and receive emails and also format them to your own style. This can be simply formatting text or adding customized stationery. To use Mail:

1 Click on the Get Mail button to download available email messages

2 Click on the New Message button to create a new email

3 Enter a recipient in the To box, a title in the Subject box and then text for the email in the main window

4 Click on the Format button to access options for formatting the text in the email

5 Click on these buttons to Reply to, Reply to All or Forward an email you have received

6 Select or open an email and click on the Delete button to remove it

Email Conversations

Within Mail you can view conversations, i.e. groups of emails on the same subject. There is also a facility for showing your own replies within a conversation. To view a conversation:

1 Select View>Organize by Conversation from the Mail menu bar

2 Emails with the same subject are grouped together as a

conversation in the left-hand pane. The number of grouped emails is shown at the right-hand side

3 Click here to view the full list of emails

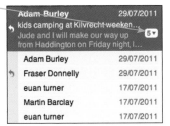

4 The full conversation is shown in the right-hand pane

5 Click on this button to include your own messages in a conversation

6 Click on this button to hide your own messages in a conversation

Attaching Photos

Emails do not have to be restricted to plain text. Through the use of attachments they can also include other documents and particularly photos. This is an excellent way to send photos to family and friends around the world. There are two ways to attach photos to an email:

Attach button

To attach photos using the Attach button:

1 Click on this icon on the Mail toolbar

146

2 Browse your hard drive for the photo(s) you want to include in your email. Select the photos you want

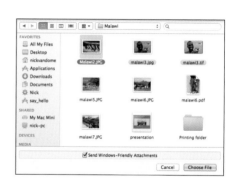

3 Click on the Choose File button

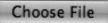

4 The photo is added to the body of the email

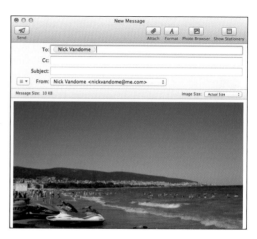

Photo Browser

To attach photos using the Photo Browser:

1 Click on this icon on the Mail toolbar

2 Browse the Photo Browser for the photo(s) that you want to include

Don't forget

The Photo Browser is available from a variety of other applications.

3 Drag the selected photo(s) into the open email to include them in the message

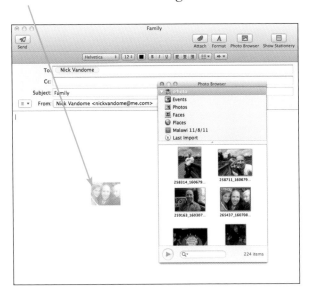

Email Stationery

You do not have to settle for conservative formatting options in emails and Mail offers a variety of templates that can give your messages a creative and eye-catching appearance. It can also be used to format any photos that you have attached to your message. This is done through the use of the Stationery function. To use this:

1 Click on this icon on the Mail toolbar

2 Select a category for the stationery

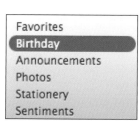

3 Double-click on a style to apply it to the email

4 The stationery incorporates any photos that have been attached from the Photo Browser

Dealing with Junk Email

Spam, or junk email, is the scourge of every email user. It consists of unwanted and unsolicited messages that are usually sent in bulk to lists of email addresses. In Mail there is a function which limits the amount of junk email that you receive in your Inbox. To do this:

1 When you receive a junk email, click on this button on the Mail toolbar (initially this will help to train Mail to identify junk email)

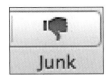

2 Once Mail has recognized the types of junk that you receive it will start to filter them directly into the Junk Mailbox

It is worth occasionally checking in your Junk Mailbox, in case something you do want has been put there.

3 To set the preferences for junk email select Mail>Preferences from the Menu bar and click on the Junk tab

4 Junk email is displayed in the Junk Mailbox

Messaging

The Messages app enables you to send text messages (iMessages) to other Mountain Lion users or those with an iPhone, iPad or iPod Touch using iOS 5, or above. It can also be used to send photos, videos and make FaceTime calls. To use Messages:

You require an Apple ID to use Messages and you will need to enter these details when you first access it. If you do not have an Apple ID you will be able to create one at this point.

1 Click on this icon on the Dock

2 Click on this button to start a new conversation

3 Click on this button and select a contact. These will be from your Contacts (address book) app. To send an iMessage the recipient has to have an Apple ID

Click on the video icon in the top right-hand corner of the Messages window to make a FaceTime call.

4 The person with whom you are having a conversation is displayed in the left-hand panel

To delete a conversation, rollover it in the left-hand panel and click on this cross.

5 The conversation continues down the right-hand panel. Click here to write a message and press Return to send it. Drag photos or videos here to include them too

9 Mac Mobility

This chapter shows how Apple has revolutionized the way we use mobile devices, including the sharing service iCloud.

iPhone

Launched in 2007, the iPhone is one of the products that has helped propel Apple to be the world's most valuable technology company. It is a smartphone that is capable of accessing the web, using email, taking photos, recording videos and playing multimedia content such as music and movies. In essence it is really a mini computer that can also be used to make phone calls and send and receive texts.

iPhone 5
The biggest thing to happen to iPhone since iPhone.

The user interface of the iPhone is a touchscreen with a virtual keypad, rather than the traditional screen and physical keypad. The screen is navigated around by using swiping gestures with your fingers and tapping to access items. The keypad appears whenever you need to input text, such as when using the Notes app, or entering a web address into the Safari web browser app.

Don't forget

The latest iPhone, iPhone 5, is thinner and lighter than previous versions and has a taller screen. It also has 4G connectivity, where this is available, for faster web access.

The iPhone partly made its name through the huge range of apps that quickly became available after its launch. These can be downloaded from the App Store and cover pretty much everything you ever wanted to do on a smartphone.

Some of the features of the latest iPhone are:

- A high resolution Retina display

- iOS 6. This is the operating system for Apple's mobile devices including the iPhone, iPad and iPod Touch

- An enhanced version of Siri, the iOS 6 voice assistant

- The new 3D Map app, designed specifically for iOS 6

- iCloud. This is an online service that enables you to store your content in the iCloud and share it between other Mac devices (see pages 155–158 for more details)

iPad

Apple has a knack of changing the way people look at computers and computing and the iPad was another product that continued this trend. It is a tablet computer that is primarily designed for multimedia content, such as movies, video games, music and books, but it can also be used for productivity options such as word processing or creating presentations and spreadsheets.

The first iPad was released in 2010 and operates in a similar way to the iPhone, with a large touchscreen and a virtual keyboard that appears when you need to type anything. All iPads come with Wi-Fi connectivity for access to the web and some models have 3G (or 4G in some locations) connectivity so that you can connect to the Internet in the same way as you would with an iPhone.

The majority of apps for the iPad can be downloaded from the App Store, in the same way as for the iPhone and Mac computers.

The current version of the iPad is The new iPad (which is the third version) and some of its features are:

- Dual-core A5X processor chip
- Two cameras, one on the front and one on the back
- Up to 10 hours battery life
- Instant On. Turns on from sleep immediately
- iOS 6 operating system
- Retina Display screen

Don't forget

A Smart Cover can be added to an iPad. This is a firm cover that protects the iPad and it can also be used to support it by folding it behind the iPad. The Smart Covers come in a range of colors.

iOS 6

iOS 6 is the latest operating system for the mobile Apple devices: iPhone, iPad and iPod Touch. Because they are required to operate differently from computers, mobile devices need a different type of operating system. However, with iOS 6 it is possible to ensure that your mobile devices can also be used in conjunction with any of your Mac computers. iOS 6 is a robust operating system that has a wealth of features for all of your mobile computing needs.

Features

Some of the features of iOS 6 are

- Enhanced Safari web browser

- Refined photo sharing with Photo Stream

- Messages. Free text and video messaging with other Mac users, either on a Mac computer or mobile device

- FaceTime video calls

- Notification Center for all of your online alerts

- Improved syncing with your email and calendar

- Apple's own 3D Map app

- Game Center for one of the best mobile gaming experiences

- A range of multi-touch gestures for accessing content

- Direct integration with Twitter and Facebook

- Integration with iCloud (see page 155) so that items you create on iOS 6 devices are readily available on other compatible Mac devices

Don't forget

The iOS 6 voice assistant, Siri, can be used to provide verbal answers to a variety of questions, by looking over your iPhone, iPad or iPod Touch and also by using a selection of web services.

About iCloud

Cloud computing is an attractive proposition and one that has gained greatly in popularity in recent years. As a concept, it consists of storing your content on an external computer server. This not only gives you added security in terms of backing up your information, it also means that the content can then be shared over a variety of mobile devices.

iCloud is Apple's consumer cloud-computing product that consists of online services such as email, a calendar, contacts and saving documents. iCloud provides users with a way to save their files and content to the online service and then use them across their Apple devices such as other Mac computers, iPhones, iPads and iPod Touches.

About iCloud

iCloud can be set up from this icon in System Preferences:

You can use iCloud to save and share the following:

- Music
- Photos
- Documents
- Apps
- Books
- Backups
- Contacts and calendars

When you save an item to the iCloud it automatically pushes it to all of your other compatible devices; you do not have to manually sync anything, iCloud does it all for you.

Don't forget

The standard iCloud service is free and this includes an iCloud email address and 5GB of online storage.

Don't forget

There is also a version of iCloud for Windows.

Setting up iCloud

To use iCloud with Mountain Lion you first need to have an Apple ID. This is a service you can register for to be able to access a range of Apple facilities, including iCloud. You can register with an email address and a password. When you first start using iCloud you will be prompted for your Apple ID details. If you do not have an Apple ID you can apply for one at this point:

Don't forget

To use iTunes and iPhoto with iCloud, you need to have iTunes 10.5, or later, and iPhoto 9.2, or later, in order to share your music and photos.

1 Sign in with your Apple ID, or

2 Click on this button to create a new one

Setting up iCloud
To use iCloud

Don't forget

Music and photos are not included in your 5GB storage limit on iCloud. This only includes emails, documents, account information, Camera Roll (for saved or edited photos) and account settings.

1 Open System Preferences and click on the iCloud button

2 Check on the items you want included within iCloud. All of these items will be backed up and shared across all of your compatible Apple devices

Using iCloud

Once iCloud has been set up in System Preferences there is relatively little that needs to be done. iCloud will take care of things in the background and back up and share all of the items that have been specified. For instance, when you create a note or a reminder it will be saved by iCloud and made available to any other Apple devices that are iCloud-enabled. Photos and documents can also be shared via iCloud.

Sharing photos

Photos can be shared via iCloud using the iPhoto app:

Don't forget

Once you have set up iCloud, you can login to the online service at www.icloud.com/ This consists of your online email service, your contacts and your calendar. You can login to your iCloud account from any Internet-enabled device.

1 When iCloud is active, a Photo Stream folder is created in iPhoto. Click on this to view its contents

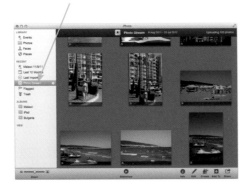

2 All of the photos in the Photo Stream will be available in other iCloud-enabled devices. Similarly, you will be able to view the Photo Streams from your other devices

Hot tip

When you import new photos into iPhoto these are added to the Photo Stream (providing you have an Internet connection). To use existing photos in iPhoto, just drag them from the main window onto the Photo Stream button.

157

...cont'd

Sharing documents

The latest versions of the Apple productivity apps (Pages, Numbers and Keynote) are optimized for use with iCloud. This means that if you create a presentation or report on, for instance, an iPad, you can also open it on a Mac running Mountain Lion (as long as you have the same apps). To share documents:

1 In the iCloud System Preferences, make sure that the Documents & Data option is checked On

2 Open one of the Apple productivity apps, such as Pages

3 Click on the iCloud button to view which documents are available in the iCloud. Click on the On My Mac button to see which documents are just on your Mac

4 Open, edit and save a document from the iCloud. The edited document will then be available on other iCloud-enabled devices

5 If you create a new document on your Mac, you can move it to the iCloud. Click here next to the document's name and click on Move To...

6 Make sure that iCloud is selected in the Where box and click on the Save button

10 Expanding Your Horizons

This chapter shows how you can develop your skills on a Mac, from adding new users to setting up a network of computers.

Adding Users

Due to the power and versatility of Macs it would seem a shame to limit their use to a single person. Thankfully, it is possible to set up user accounts for several people on the same Mac. This means that each person can log in to their own settings and preferences. All user accounts can be password protected, to ensure that each user's environment is secure. To set up multiple user accounts:

1 Click on the System Preferences icon on the Dock

2 Click on the Users & Groups icon

Users & Groups

Don't forget

Each user can select their own icon or photo of themselves.

3 The information about the current account is displayed. This is your own account and the information is based on details you provided when you first set up your Mac

4 Click on this icon to enable new accounts to be added (the padlock needs to be open)

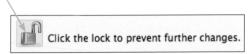

Click the lock to prevent further changes.

5 Click on the plus sign icon to add a new account

6 Enter the details for the new account holder

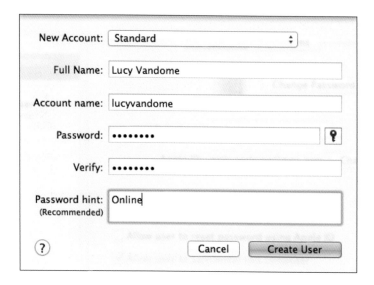

Don't forget

By default, you are the administrator of your own Mac. This means that you can create, edit and delete other user accounts.

7 Click on the Create User button

Create User

8 The new account is added to the list in the Accounts window, under Other Users

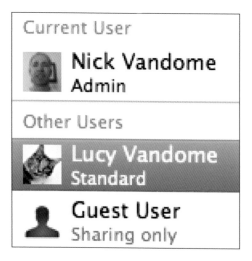

Current User

Nick Vandome
Admin

Other Users

Lucy Vandome
Standard

Guest User
Sharing only

Login Options

Once you have set up more than one user you can determine what happens at login, i.e. when the Mac is turned on. You may want to display a list of all of the users for that machine, or you may want to have yourself logged in automatically. To set login options:

1 Click on the System Preferences icon on the Dock

2 Click on the Users & Groups icon

3 Click on the padlock to open it

4 Click on the Login Options button

5 The Login Options window allows you to select settings for when you turn on your Mac

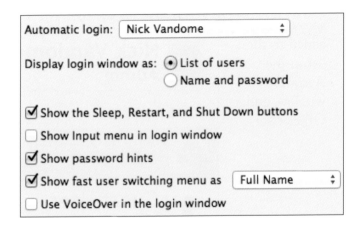

6 Click on the Automatic login box

7 Select a name from the list. (If Off is selected all of the users for that Mac will be displayed at login)

Off

✓ Nick Vandome

Lucy Vandome

If Automatic login is selected for a named user, no username or password needs to be selected when the Mac is turned on.

8 If Off is selected, select one of the options for how the login window is displayed

Display login window as: ● List of users
                        ○ Name and password

9 Check on this box if you want to make it as easy as possible to switch between users (see page 164)

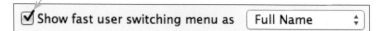

Switching Between Users

If there are multiple users set up on a Mac it is useful to be able to switch between them as quickly as possible.
When this is done, the first user's session is retained so that they can return to it if required. To switch between users:

1 Make sure Fast User Switching is enabled (see page 163)

☑ Show fast user switching menu as ⬚ Full Name ⬍

2 At the top-right of the screen, click on the current user's name

Nick Vandome

Don't forget

When you switch between users, the first user remains logged in and their current session is retained intact.

164

3 Click on the name of another user

rged) Sun 17:05 **Nick Vandome**

Lucy Vandome

⊘ Nick Vandome

4 Enter the relevant password (if required)

Lucy Vandome

•••••••• ➔

5 Click on the arrow to login

Parental Controls

Children, and grandchildren, love computers and it is not always possible to fully monitor what they are doing on them. Therefore, it is useful to be able to put in some system controls if you have any user accounts for younger members of the family. To do this:

1 Click on the System Preferences icon on the Dock

2 Click on the Parental Controls icon

Don't forget

Different types of parental controls can be set for each user account on a Mac.

3 Select a user account to which you want to apply controls. By default, Parental Controls are turned off

4 Check on this button to enable Parental Controls in the Users & Groups System Preferences

...cont'd

Apps controls

1 Click on the Apps tab

2 Check on the Use Simple Finder box to show a simplified version of the Finder

3 Check on this box if you want to limit the types of app that a user can access

Don't forget

If only certain apps are allowed, others will be visible but the user will not be able to open any of them.

4 Check off the boxes next to the types of apps that you do not want used

5 Click here to select options for age limits in terms of access items in the App Store

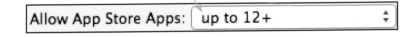

Web controls

1 Click on the Web tab

2 Check on this button to try to prevent access to websites with adult content

3 Check on this button to specify specific websites that are suitable to be viewed

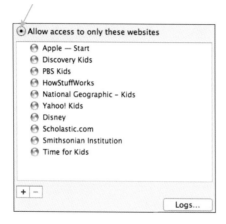

People controls

1 Click on the People tab

2 Check on the boxes to limit the type of content in email messages, games and text messages

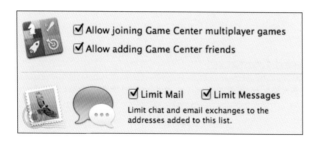

...cont'd

3 The Allowed Contacts box enables you to enter details of people who you want to allow to contact the user via email or iMessages

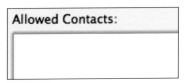

4 Click on this button to add new contacts

5 Enter details of the contacts or click on this button to access contacts in your address book

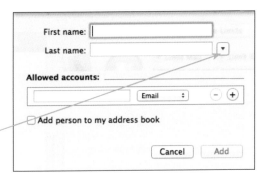

6 Select a contact and click on the Add button

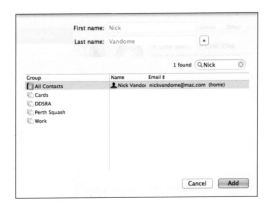

7 The selected contact is displayed in the Allowed Contacts window

Time controls

1 Click on the Time Limits tab   **Time Limits**

2 Check on this box to limit the amount of time the user can use the Mac for during weekdays

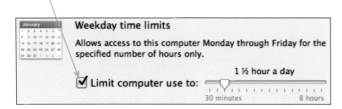

Weekday time limits

Allows access to this computer Monday through Friday for the specified number of hours only.

1 ½ hour a day

Limit computer use to:

30 minutes   8 hours

3 Check on this box to limit the amount of time the user can use the Mac for during weekends

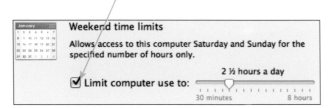

Weekend time limits

Allows access to this computer Saturday and Sunday for the specified number of hours only.

2 ½ hours a day

Limit computer use to:

30 minutes   8 hours

4 Check on these boxes to determine the times at which the user cannot access their account

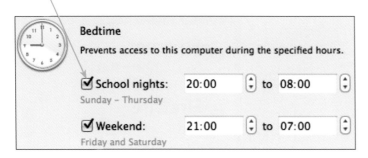

Bedtime

Prevents access to this computer during the specified hours.

School nights: 20:00   to   08:00
Sunday – Thursday

Weekend: 21:00   to   07:00
Friday and Saturday

Creating Your Own Network

Computer networks are two or more computers joined together to share information. A computer connected to the Internet constitutes a network, as does one computer connected to another.

Networks can be set up by joining computers together with cables or wirelessly. The latter is becoming more and more common and this can be done with a wireless router and a wireless card in the computer. New Macs come with wireless cards installed so it is just a case of buying a wireless router. (Apple sells its own version of this, known as AirPort.) A wireless router connects to your telephone line and then you can set up your Mac, or Macs, to join the network and communicate with each other and the Internet. To do this:

1 Click on the System Preferences icon on the Dock

2 Click on the Network icon

3 The Network window displays the current settings

4 Click on the Assist Me button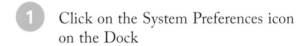

5 The Network Setup Assistant is launched

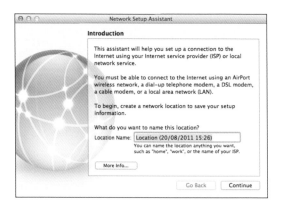

6 Enter a name for your network connection

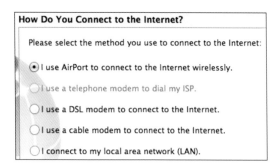

7 Click on the Continue button

Continue

8 Select how you connect to the Internet

How Do You Connect to the Internet?

Please select the method you use to connect to the Internet:

⦿ I use AirPort to connect to the Internet wirelessly.

○ I use a telephone modem to dial my ISP.

○ I use a DSL modem to connect to the Internet.

○ I use a cable modem to connect to the Internet.

○ I connect to my local area network (LAN).

9 Click on the Continue button

Continue

...cont'd

10 Select the name of your wireless router

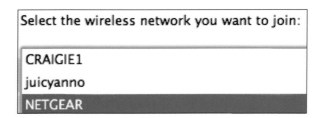

Select the wireless network you want to join:

CRAIGIE1

juicyanno

NETGEAR

11 Enter the password for the router. This will have been set when you installed the router

Password: Selected network requires a password

••••••••

12 Click on the Continue button   **Continue**

13 The Ready to Connect window confirms that you are ready to connect to your router

14 Click on the Continue button   **Continue**

Sharing on a Network

One of the main reasons for creating a network of two or more computers is to share files between them.
On networked Macs this involves setting them up so that they can share files, and then accessing these files.

Setting up file sharing

To set up file sharing on a networked Mac:

1 Click on the System Preference icon on the Dock

2 Click on the Sharing icon

3 Check on the boxes next to the items you want to share (the most common items to share are files and printers)

Don't forget

If you only use your network to connect to the Internet then you do not need to worry about file sharing. This is mainly for sharing files between two different computers.

4 Click on the padlock to close it and prevent more changes

...cont'd

Accessing other computers

When you access other computers on a network you do so as either a registered user or a guest. If you are a registered user it usually means you are accessing another computer of which you are an administrator i.e. the main user. This gives you greater access to the computer's contents than if you are a guest. To access another computer on your network:

1 Networked computers should show up automatically in the Finder. Double-click on one to access it

2 By default, you will be connected as a Guest, with limited access. Click on the Connect As... button in the Finder window

3 Click on Registered User button

4 Enter your name and the password for the computer to which you want to connect (this will be your user password on that computer)

5 Click on the Connect button

6 In the Finder you will have access to the hard drive of the networked computer

7 You will then be able to access files and folders in the same way as if they were on the computer on which you are viewing them

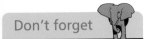

Don't forget

When connecting to another computer, it has to be turned on.

Guest users

Guest users on a network are users other than yourself, or other registered users, to whom you want to limit access to your files and folders. Guests only have access to a folder called the Drop Box in your own Public folder. To share files with Guest users you have to first copy them into the Drop Box. To do this:

1 Create a file and select File>Save from the Menu bar

2 Navigate to your own home folder (this is created automatically by OS X and displayed in the Finder Sidebar)

Don't forget

Your home folder is the one with your Mac username.

3 Double-click on the Public folder

4 Double-click on the Drop Box folder

5 Save the file into the Drop Box

...cont'd

Accessing a Drop Box
To access files in a Drop Box:

1 Double-click on a networked computer in the Finder

2 Click on the Connect As button in the Finder window

3 Click on the Guest button

4 Click on the Connect button

5 Double-click on the administrator's folder

6 Double-click on the Drop Box folder to access the files within it

11 Safety Net

This chapter shows some of the ways in which you can keep your Mac, and your files, safe and secure.

Mac Security

Modern computers are plagued by viruses, spyware and malware, all of which can corrupt data or impair the smooth running of the system. Thankfully, Macs are less prone to this than computers running Windows, partly due to the fact that there are a smaller number of Macs for the virus writers to worry about and partly because the UNIX system, on which the Mac OS X is based, is a very robust platform.

However, this is not to say that Mac users should be complacent in the face of potential attacks. In order to minimize the threat of viruses and unwanted visitors try some of the following steps:

- Install anti-virus software and a firewall. Although this is not as essential as for a computer running Windows it will give you additional peace of mind. Norton and Sophos produce good anti-virus software for the Mac

- Protect your Mac with a password. This means that no-one can login without the required password

- Download software updates from Apple, which, among other things, contain security updates (see page 179)

- Do not open suspicious email attachments

- In Safari, select Safari>Preferences and click on the Security tab. Deselect any items that you feel may put your computer at risk

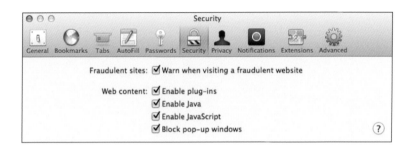

Hot tip

Mountain Lion has a security feature, known as Gatekeeper, that enables you to specify details about apps that are downloaded to your Mac. This can be from anywhere, the App Store and identified developers, or just from the App Store. This feature is found in the Security & Privacy System Preference, under the General tab.

Updating Software

Apple periodically releases updates for its apps and the OS X operating system. All of these are now available through the App Store. To update software:

1 Open System Preferences and click on the Software Update icon

2 Click here to select options for how you are notified about updates and how they are downloaded

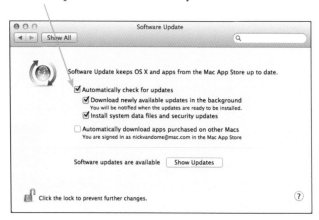

3 If updates are available, click on the Show Updates button

4 Available updates are shown in the Updates section in the App Store. Click on the Update buttons to update the selected apps

179

Don't forget

If automatic updates is selected, you will be alerted at the appropriate time when updates are available. This is done through the Notification Center.

Hot tip

Check on the 'Automatically download apps purchased on other Macs' box if you want to activate this function.

Don't forget

For some software updates, such as those to OS X itself, you may have to restart your computer for them to take effect.

Checking Your System

Macs have a couple of apps that can be used to check the overall health and condition of your system. These are utilities called Activity Monitor and System Information. To access these apps:

1 In the Finder click on the Applications button or access it from the Launchpad

2 Double-click on the Utilities folder

3 Double-click on either app to open it

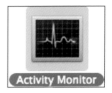

Activity Monitor

This can be used to check how much memory is being used up on your Mac, and also by certain apps:

1 Click on the CPU tab to see how much processor memory is being used up

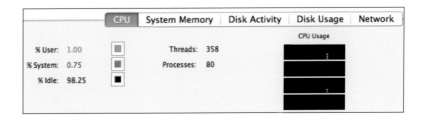

2 Click on the System Memory tab to see how much system memory (RAM) is being used up

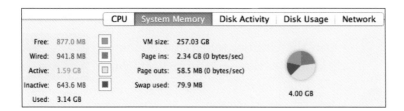

Don't forget

RAM is the memory that is used to open and run apps.
The more RAM you have, the more efficiently your Mac will run.

3 Click on the Disk Usage tab to see how much space has been taken up on the hard drive

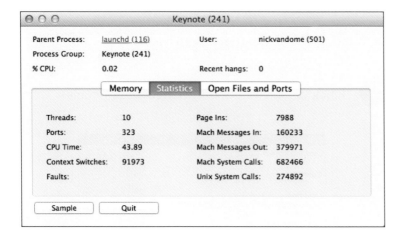

4 Double-click on an app to see its individual details

...cont'd

System Information
This can be used to view how the different hardware and software elements on your Mac are performing. To do this:

1 Open the Utilities folder and double-click on the System Information icon

2 Click on the Hardware link and click on an item of hardware

▼ Hardware
  ATA
  Audio (Built In)
  Bluetooth
  Card Reader
  Diagnostics
  Disc Burning

3 Details about the item of hardware, and its performance, are displayed

MATSHITA DVD-R UJ-898:

Firmware Revision:	HE13
Interconnect:	ATAPI
Burn Support:	Yes (Apple Shipping Drive)
Cache:	1024 KB
Reads DVD:	Yes
CD-Write:	-R, -RW
DVD-Write:	-R, -R DL, -RW, +R, +R DL, +RW
Write Strategies:	CD-TAO, CD-SAO, DVD-DAO
Media:	To show the available burn speeds, insert a disc and choose View > Refresh

4 Click on software items to view their details

Calendar	6.0
Canon IJ Printer Utility	7.27.0

Calendar:

Version:	6.0
Last Modified:	23/06/2012 08:26
Kind:	Intel
64-Bit (Intel):	Yes
App Store:	No
Location:	/Applications/Calendar.app

Dealing with Crashes

Although Macs are known for their stability, there are occasions when something goes wrong and an app crashes or freezes. This is usually denoted by a spinning, colored ball (known as the "Spinning Beach Ball of Death"). Only rarely will you have to turn off your Mac and turn it on again to resolve the problem. Usually, Force Quit can be used to close down the affected app. To do this:

1 Once the spinning ball appears, click on the Apple Menu

2 Select Force Quit from the Apple Menu

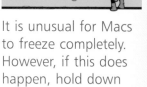

or

1 Hold down the Command (Apple), Alt and Esc keys at the same time

2 Select the non-responding app

3 Click on the Force Quit button

Don't forget

It is unusual for Macs to freeze completely. However, if this does happen, hold down the start button for a few seconds until your Mac turns off. You should then be able to start it normally.

183

Backing Up

Backing up data is a chore, but it is an essential one: if the worst comes to the worst and all of your data is corrupted or lost then you will be very grateful that you went to the trouble of backing it up. Macs have a number of options for backing up data.

Burning discs

One of the most traditional methods of backing up data is to burn it onto a disc that can then be stored elsewhere. These days this is most frequently done on CDs or DVDs. To do this:

1 Insert the CD/DVD into the CD/DVD slot

2 Select for the disc to be shown in the Finder

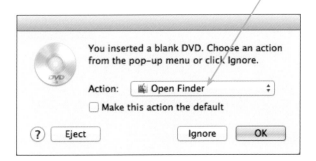

You inserted a blank DVD. Choose an action from the pop-up menu or click Ignore.

Action: Open Finder

Make this action the default

Eject   Ignore   OK

3 Locate the item you want to copy

Pictures

4 Drag it onto the disc name in the Finder

5 Click on this icon to burn the disc

Time Machine

Time Machine is a feature of OS X that gives you great peace of mind. In conjunction with an external hard drive, it creates a backup of your whole system, including folders, files, apps and even the OS X operating system itself.

Once it has been set up, Time Machine takes a backup every hour and you can then go into Time Machine to restore any files that have been deleted or become corrupt.

Setting up Time Machine

To use Time Machine it has to first be set up. This involves attaching a hard drive to your Mac. To set up Time Machine:

1 Click on the Time Machine icon on the Dock or access it in the System Preferences

2 You will be prompted to set up Time Machine

3 Click on the Set Up Time Machine button

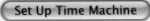

4 In the Time Machine System Preferences window, click on the Choose Backup Disk... button

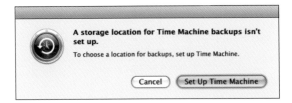

Beware

If an external hard drive is not attached to your Mac you will not be able to use Time Machine and a warning message will appear when you try to set it up.

185

...cont'd

5 Connect an external hard drive and select it

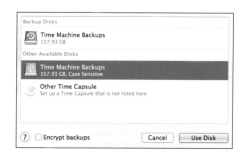

6 Click on the Use for Backup button

7 In the Time Machine System Preferences window, drag the button to the On position

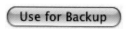

8 The backup will begin. The initial backup copies your whole system and can take several hours. Subsequent hourly backups only look at items that have been changed since the previous backup

9 The progress of the backup is displayed in the System Preferences window and also here:

Index

N

O

P